ALSO BY SEAMUS HEANEY

AENEID BOOK VI

AENEID BOOK VI

A NEW VERSE TRANSLATION

BILINGUAL EDITION

SEAMUS HEANEY

FARRAR, STRAUS AND GIROUX   NEW YORK

Farrar, Straus and Giroux
18 West 18th Street, New York 10011

Printed in the United States of America
English translation originally published in 2016 by
    Faber and Faber Limited, Great Britain
Bilingual edition published by Farrar, Straus and Giroux
First bilingual edition, 2016

Library of Congress Cataloging-in-Publication Data
Names: Virgil, author. | Heaney, Seamus, 1939–2013 translator. | Virgil.
    Aeneis. Liber 6. | Virgil. Aeneis. Liber 6. English.
Title: Aeneid Book VI : a new verse translation / Seamus Heaney [translator].
Description: First edition. | New York : Farrar, Straus and Giroux, 2016. |
    English and Latin (bilingual text).
Identifiers: LCCN 2015044475 | ISBN 9780374104191 (hardback) |
    ISBN 9780374715359 (e-book)
Subjects: LCSH: Aeneas (Legendary character)—Poetry. | Voyages to the
    otherworld—Poetry. | Epic poetry, Latin—Translations into English. |
    BISAC: POETRY / English, Irish, Scottish, Welsh. | POETRY / Epic.
Classification: LCC PA6807.A5 .H436 2016 | DDC 873/.01—dc23
LC record available at http://lccn.loc.gov/2015044475

Designed by Jonathan D. Lippincott

Our books may be purchased in bulk for promotional, educational, or
business use. Please contact your local bookseller or the Macmillan Corporate
and Premium Sales Department at 1-800-221-7945, extension 5442, or by
e-mail at MacmillanSpecialMarkets@macmillan.com.

www.fsgbooks.com
www.twitter.com/fsgbooks • www.facebook.com/fsgbooks

10 9 8 7 6 5 4 3 2 1

CONTENTS

TRANSLATOR'S NOTE

This translation of *Aeneid* VI is neither a "version" nor a crib: it is more like classics homework, the result of a lifelong desire to honour the memory of my Latin teacher at St. Columb's College, Father Michael McGlinchey, about whom I wrote briefly in the prefatory note to *The Golden Bough* (in de Bonnefant & Imprenta de los Trópicos, 1992). The set text for our A-level exam in 1957 was *Aeneid* IX but McGlinchey was forever sighing, "Och, boys, I wish it were Book VI." Over the years, therefore, I gravitated towards that part of the poem and took special note of it after my father died, since the story it tells is that of Aeneas' journey to meet the shade of his father Anchises in the land of the dead. But the impulse to go ahead with a rendering of the complete book arrived in 2007, as the result of a sequence of poems written to greet the birth of a first granddaughter.

The autobiographical sequence in twelve sections, published in *Human Chain* (2010), was entitled "Route 110" and plotted incidents from my own life against certain well-known episodes in Book VI: thus a bus inspector's direction of passengers to the bus for Route 110—the one I often took from Belfast to my home in County Derry—paralleled the moment when Charon directs the shades on board his barge to cross the Styx; and a memory of the wake of a drowned neighbour whose body was not retrieved for three days shadowed the case of Aeneas' drowned, unburied helmsman Palinurus. It was a matter, in other words, of a relatively simple "mythic method" being employed over the twelve sections. The focus this time, however, was not the meeting of the son with the father, but the vision of future Roman generations with which Book VI ends, specifically the moment on the bank of the river Lethe where we are shown the souls of those about to be reborn and return to life on earth.

"Route 110" also ends with birth and the whole sequence is dedicated to "one / Whose long wait on the shaded bank has ended." And so, elated and inspired by having completed the sequence in thanksgiving for that infant birth, and in memory of the man who first turned my ear and temperament to Virgil, I began work on a complete translation of Book VI. Yet as anyone familiar with this work knows, the beginning and middle of that book are alive with poetic and narrative energy, but not so the ending. By the time the story reaches its climax in Anchises' vision of a glorious Roman race who will issue from Aeneas' marriage with Lavinia, the translator is likely to have moved from inspiration to grim determination: the roll call of generals and imperial heroes, the allusions to variously famous or obscure historical victories and defeats, make this part of the poem something of a test for reader and translator alike. But for the sake of the little one whose "earthlight" broke in late 2006, and the one who sighed for his favourite Virgil in that 1950s classroom, it had to be gone through with.

Michael McGlinchey created an inner literalist who still hunts for the main verb of a sentence and still, to the best of his ability, disentangles the subordinate clauses, although usually nowadays with the help of a crib from the Loeb Library or the old Penguin Classics. Yet nowadays too that sixth-form homunculus must contend with a different supervisor, a writer of verse who has things other than literal accuracy on his mind and in his ear: rhythm and metre and lineation, the voice and its pacing, the need for a diction decorous enough for Virgil but not so antique as to sound out of tune with a more contemporary idiom— all the fleeting, fitful anxieties that afflict the literary translator.

Seamus Heaney

AENEID BOOK VI

Sic fatur lacrimans classique immittit habenas,
et tandem Euboicis Cumarum adlabitur oris.
obvertunt pelago proras, tum dente tenaci
ancora fundabat navis, et litora curvae
praetexunt puppes. iuvenum manus emicat ardens
litus in Hesperium; quaerit pars semina flammae
abstrusa in venis silicis, pars densa ferarum
tecta rapit silvas, inventaque flumina monstrat.
at pius Aeneas arces, quibus altus Apollo
10   praesidet, horrendaeque procul secreta Sibyllae,
antrum immane, petit, magnam cui mentem animumque
Delius inspirat vates aperitque futura.

In tears as he speaks, Aeneas loosens out sail
And gives the whole fleet its head, so now at last
They ride ashore on the waves at Euboean Cumae.
There they turn round the ships to face out to sea.
Anchors bite deep, craft are held fast, curved
Sterns cushion on sand, prows frill the beach.
Now a band of young hotbloods vaults quickly out
On to the shore of Italia, some after flint
For the seedling fire it hides in its veins,
10   Some crashing through woodland thickets, the haunts
Of wild beasts, pointing amazed at new rivers.
But Aeneas, devoted as ever, has taken the road
Up towards a fort, the high seat of Apollo,
Then on to a place apart, a vast scaresome cavern,
The Sibyl's deep-hidden retreat. There the god breathes
Into her, overwhelmingly, knowledge and vision,
Opening her eyes to the future. Before long

iam subeunt Triviae lucos atque aurea tecta.

      Daedalus, ut fama est, fugiens Minoia regna,
praepetibus pinnis ausus se credere caelo,
insuetum per iter gelidas enavit ad Arctos
Chalcidicaque levis tandem super adstitit arce.
redditus his primum terris tibi, Phoebe, sacravit
remigium alarum posuitque immania templa.
20   in foribus letum Androgeo; tum pendere poenas
Cecropidae iussi, miserum! septena quotannis
corpora natorum; stat ductis sortibus urna.
contra elata mari respondet Cnosia tellus:
hic crudelis amor tauri suppostaque furto
Pasiphae mixtumque genus prolesque biformis
Minotaurus inest, Veneris monumenta nefandae;
hic labor ille domus et inextricabilis error;
magnum reginae sed enim miseratus amorem

They pass through the golden precincts and groves
Of Diana, the goddess of crossroads.

20   And now they pause on that hill where Dedalus,
At the end of his flight, first fluttered to earth:
He had risked himself to the sky, away and afloat
To the north, through the cold air, unprecedented,
Rowing with wings—which he then dedicated
To you, Phoebus Apollo, there on the spot
Where he landed, and built in your honour
A mighty temple, the doors of it decorated
With scenes in relief.

                 First the death of Androgeos.

30   Then the stricken Athenians, doomed to deliver
Seven grown-up sons for sacrifice every year.
There too stood the empty urn, from which
Only now the fatal lots had been drawn.
On the opposite leaf, the land of Knossos
Rising out of the sea: here was the horn-cruel bull
With Pasiphaë under him (a congress
Her cunning arranged), whence would be born
The Minotaur, crossbreed and offspring
Of abominable desire.

40   Also shown:
The bewildering, intricate maze—
Never got through until Dedalus, out of pity
For infatuated Ariadne,
Guided a prince's blind footsteps

5

Daedalus ipse dolos tecti ambagesque resolvit,
30 caeca regens filo vestigia. tu quoque magnam
partem opere in tanto, sineret dolor, Icare, haberes;
bis conatus erat casus effingere in auro,
bis patriae cecidere manus. quin protinus omnia
perlegerent oculis, ni iam praemissus Achates
adforet atque una Phoebi Triviaeque sacerdos,
Deiphobe Glauci, fatur quae talia regi:
"non hoc ista sibi tempus spectacula poscit:
nunc grege de intacto septem mactare iuvencos
praestiterit, totidem lectas de more bidentis."
40 talibus adfata Aenean (nec sacra morantur
iussa viri) Teucros vocat alta in templa sacerdos.

Excisum Euboicae latus ingens rupis in antrum,
quo lati ducunt aditus centum, ostia centum,
unde ruunt totidem voces, responsa Sibyllae.
ventum erat ad limen, cum virgo, "poscere fata

With a payout of thread, past every wrong turn
And every dead end he himself had devised
And constructed.

        In which grand design
You too would figure significantly,
50   Icarus, had sorrow allowed it. Twice
Dedalus tried to model your fall in gold, twice
His hands, the hands of a father, failed him.

The Trojans would have kept standing, fascinated
By all on display, except that just then Achates,
Who'd been sent on ahead, came back accompanied
By the Sibyl, Deiphobe, daughter of Glaucus, priestess
Of Diana and Phoebus. Who addressed the prince:
"This is no time to be standing staring here.
It would be better now to pick out for sacrifice
60   Seven bullocks from a herd that has not been yoked,
And an equal number of properly chosen ewes."
Having spoken these words to Aeneas (whose men
Are quick to obey her instructions) the priestess
Summons the Trojans into her high inner sanctum.

At Cumae, behind the broad cliff, an enormous cave
Has been quarried: a hundred entrances, a hundred
Wide-open mouths lead in, and out of them scramble
A hundred echoing voices, the Sibyl's responses.
They arrived at that threshold and the vestal cried,
70   "Now! Now you must ask what your fate is. The god

tempus" ait: "deus, ecce, deus!" cui talia fanti
ante fores subito non vultus, non color unus,
non comptae mansere comae, sed pectus anhelum,
et rabie fera corda tument, maiorque videri

50   nec mortale sonans, adflata est numine quando
iam propiore dei. "cessas in vota precesque,
Tros," ait, "Aenea? cessas? neque enim ante dehiscent
attonitae magna ora domus." et talia fata
conticuit. gelidus Teucris per dura cucurrit
ossa tremor, funditque preces rex pectore ab imo:
"Phoebe, gravis Troiae semper miserate labores,
Dardana qui Paridis derexti tela manusque
corpus in Aeacidae, magnas obeuntia terras
tot maria intravi duce te penitusque repostas

60   Massylum gentes praetentaque Syrtibus arva;
iam tandem Italiae fugientis prendimus oras;
hac Troiana tenus fuerit fortuna secuta.
vos quoque Pergameae iam fas est parcere genti,
dique deaeque omnes, quibus obstitit Ilium et ingens
gloria Dardaniae. tuque, o sanctissima vates,
praescia venturi, da (non indebita posco

Is here with us! Apollo!" Her countenance suddenly
Paled and convulsed, hair got dishevelled,
Breast was aheave, heart beating wilder and wilder.
Before their eyes she grows tall, something not mortal
Enters, she is changed by the breath of the god
Breathing through her. "Aeneas of Troy," she demands,
"Your vows and your prayers, why do you wait? Pray,
For until you have prayed, the jaws of this cavern
Won't echo or open." And there she fell silent.

80 The hardy Trojans feel a cold shiver go through them,
Their prince from the depths of his heart beseeches
The god:

        "Phoebus, you always had pity for Troy
And her troubles, it was you who steadied
Paris' aim and directed the arrow
Into Achilles, you who were pilot
As I entered sea after sea, skirting the coasts
Of distant land masses, remotest Massylia,
The sandbanked Syrtian gulfs. Here then at last

90 We set foot on Italia that seemed for so long
The unreachable: henceforth let Trojan ill fortune
Be a thing of the past. For now, all you gods
And goddesses, you to whom Troy's name and fame
Gave affront, divine law constrains you
To spare us, the last of its relics. And you,
Seeress most holy, to whom the future lies open,
Grant what I ask (no more in the end than my fate
Has assigned): home ground for my people

regna meis fatis) Latio considere Teucros

errantisque deos agitataque numina Troiae.

tum Phoebo et Triviae solido de marmore templum

70 instituam festosque dies de nomine Phoebi.

te quoque magna manent regnis penetralia nostris.

hic ego namque tuas sortes arcanaque fata

dicta meae genti ponam, lectosque sacrabo,

alma, viros. foliis tantum ne carmina manda,

ne turbata volent rapidis ludibria ventis;

ipsa canas oro." finem dedit ore loquendi.

    At Phoebi nondum patiens, immanis in antro

bacchatur vates, magnum si pectore possit

excussisse deum; tanto magis ille fatigat

80 os rabidum, fera corda domans, fingitque premendo.

ostia iamque domus patuere ingentia centum

sponte sua vatisque ferunt responsa per auras:

"o tandem magnis pelagi defuncte periclis

(sed terrae graviora manent), in regna Lavini

Dardanidae venient (mitte hanc de pectore curam);

sed non et venisse volent. bella, horrida bella

et Thybrim multo spumantem sanguine cerno.

In Latium, refuge for our wandering gods

100 And all Troy ever held sacred. Then to Phoebus

Apollo, and Diana, I will set up a temple

In solid marble and inaugurate feast days

In the god's honour. And for you, O all gracious one,

A sanctuary will be established, a vault

Where I shall preserve divinations from lots

And oracles you'll have vouchsafed to my people;

And in your service I shall ordain chosen men.

Yet one thing I ask of you: not to inscribe

Your visions in verse on the leaves

110 In case they go frolicking off

In the wind. Chant them yourself, I beseech you."

So saying, Aeneas fell silent.

Meanwhile, the Sibyl,

Resisting possession, storms through the cavern,

In the throes of her struggle with Phoebus

Apollo. But the more she froths at the mouth

And contorts, the more he controls her, commands her

And makes her his creature. Then of their own accord

Those hundred vast tunnel-mouths gape and give vent

120 To the prophetess's responses:

"O you who survived,

In the end, the sea's dangers (though worse still await

On the land), you and your Trojans will come

Into your own in Lavinium: have no fear of that.

But the day is one you will rue. I see wars,

Atrocious wars, and the Tiber surging with blood.

11

non Simois tibi nec Xanthus nec Dorica castra
defuerint; alius Latio iam partus Achilles,
90 natus et ipse dea; nec Teucris addita Iuno
usquam aberit, cum tu supplex in rebus egenis
quas gentes Italum aut quas non oraveris urbes!
causa mali tanti coniunx iterum hospita Teucris
externique iterum thalami . . .
tu ne cede malis, sed contra audentior ito,
qua tua te Fortuna sinet. via prima salutis,
quod minime reris, Graia pandetur ab urbe."
     Talibus ex adyto dictis Cumaea Sibylla
horrendas canit ambages antroque remugit,
100 obscuris vera involvens; ea frena furenti
concutit et stimulos sub pectore vertit Apollo.
 ut primum cessit furor et rabida ora quierunt,
incipit Aeneas heros: "non ulla laborum,
o virgo, nova mi facies inopinave surgit;
omnia praecepi atque animo mecum ante peregi.
unum oro: quando hic inferni ianua regis
dicitur et tenebrosa palus Acheronte refuso,

A second Simois river, a second Xanthus,
A second enemy camp lie ahead. And already
In Latium a second Achilles comes forth, he too
130   The son of a goddess. Nor will Trojans ever be free
Of Juno's harassments, while you, without allies,
Dependent, will go through Italia petitioning
Cities and peoples. And again the cause of such pain
And disaster for Trojans will be as before: a bride
Culled in a host country, an outlander groom.
But whatever disasters befall, do not flinch.
Go all the bolder to face them, follow your fate
To the limit. A road will open to safety
From the last place you would expect: a city of Greeks."

140   Thus from her innermost shrine the Sibyl of Cumae
Chanted menacing riddles and made the cave echo
With sayings where truths and enigmas were twined
Inextricably, while Apollo reined in her spasms
And curbed her, or sank the spurs in her ribs.

Then as her fit passed away and her raving went quiet,
Heroic Aeneas began: "No ordeal, O Sibyl, no new
Test can dismay me, for I have foreseen
And foresuffered all. But one thing I pray for
Especially: since here the gate opens, they say,
150   To the King of the Underworld's realms, and here
In these shadowy marshes the Acheron floods
To the surface, vouchsafe me one look,

ire ad conspectum cari genitoris et ora
contingat; doceas iter et sacra ostia pandas.
110 illum ego per flammas et mille sequentia tela
eripui his umeris medioque ex hoste recepi;
ille meum comitatus iter maria omnia mecum
atque omnis pelagique minas caelique ferebat,
invalidus, vires ultra sortemque senectae.
quin, ut te supplex peterem et tua limina adirem,
idem orans mandata dabat. gnatique patrisque,
alma, precor, miserere; potes namque omnia, nec te
nequiquam lucis Hecate praefecit Avernis.
si potuit Manis accersere coniugis Orpheus
120 Threicia fretus cithara fidibusque canoris;
si fratrem Pollux alterna morte redemit
itque reditque viam totiens—quid Thesea, magnum
quid memorem Alciden?—et mi genus ab Iove summo."
        Talibus orabat dictis arasque tenebat,
cum sic orsa loqui vates: "sate sanguine divum,
Tros Anchisiade, facilis descensus Averno:
noctes atque dies patet atri ianua Ditis;
sed revocare gradum superasque evadere ad auras,
hoc opus, hic labor est. pauci, quos aequus amavit
130 Iuppiter aut ardens evexit ad aethera virtus,
dis geniti potuere. tenent media omnia silvae,

One face-to-face meeting with my dear father.
Point out the road, open the holy doors wide.
On these shoulders I bore him through flames
And a thousand enemy spears. In the thick of fighting
I saved him, and he was at my side then
On all my sea-crossings, battling tempests and tides,
A man in old age, worn out, not meant for duress.
160   He too it was who half-prayed and half-ordered me
To make this approach, to find and petition you.
Wherefore have pity, O most gracious one,
On a son and a father, for you have the power,
You whom Hecate named mistress of wooded Avernus.
If Orpheus could call back the shade of a wife
By trusting and tuning the strings of his Thracian lyre,
If Pollux could win back a brother by taking the road
Repeatedly in and out of the land of the dead,
If Theseus and Hercules too . . . But why speak of them?
170   I myself am of highest birth, a descendant of Jove."

He was praying like that and holding on to the altar
When the Sibyl started to speak: "Blood relation
Of gods, Trojan, son of Anchises,
It is easy to descend into Avernus.
Death's dark door stands open day and night.
But to retrace your steps and get back to upper air,
That is the task, that is the undertaking.
Only a few have prevailed, sons of gods
Whom Jupiter favoured, or heroes exalted to glory
180   By their own worth. At the centre it is all forest

15

Cocytusque sinu labens circumvenit atro.
quod si tantus amor menti, si tanta cupido est
bis Stygios innare lacus, bis nigra videre
Tartara, et insano iuvat indulgere labori,
accipe quae peragenda prius. latet arbore opaca
aureus et foliis et lento vimine ramus,
Iunoni infernae dictus sacer; hunc tegit omnis
lucus et obscuris claudunt convallibus umbrae.
140 sed non ante datur telluris operta subire,
auricomos quam quis decerpserit arbore fetus.
hoc sibi pulchra suum ferri Proserpina munus
instituit; primo avulso non deficit alter
aureus, et simili frondescit virga metallo.
ergo alte vestiga oculis et rite repertum
carpe manu; namque ipse volens facilisque sequetur,
si te fata vocant; aliter non viribus ullis
vincere nec duro poteris convellere ferro.
praeterea iacet exanimum tibi corpus amici
150 (heu! nescis) totamque incestat funere classem,
dum consulta petis nostroque in limine pendes.

And a ring of dark waters, the river Cocytus, furls
And flows round it. Still, if love so torments you,
If your need to be ferried twice across the Styx
And twice to explore that deep dark abyss
Is so overwhelming, if you will and must go
That far, understand what else you must do.
Hid in the thick of a tree is a golden bough,
Gold to the tips of its leaves and the base of its stem,
Sacred (tradition declares) to the queen of that place.
190 It is safe there, roofed in by forests, in the pathless
Shadowy valleys. No one is ever allowed
Down to earth's hidden places unless he has first
Plucked this sprout of fledged gold from its tree
And handed it over to fair Proserpina
To whom it belongs, by decree, her own special gift.
And when it is plucked, a second one grows every time
In its place, golden again, emanating
That same sheen and shimmer. Therefore look up
And search deep, and as soon as you find it
200 Take hold of it boldly and duly. If fate has called you,
The bough will come away in your hand.
Otherwise, no strength you muster will break it,
Nor the hardest forged blade lop it off.

"But while you linger here on my doorstep,
Consulting and suing, sad news, alas,
Awaits: the body of one of your friends
Lies emptied of life, and his death pollutes

sedibus hunc refer ante suis et conde sepulcro.

duc nigras pecudes; ea prima piacula sunto.

sic demum lucos Stygis et regna invia vivis

aspicies." dixit pressoque obmutuit ore.

Aeneas maesto defixus lumina vultu

ingreditur, linquens antrum, caecosque volutat

eventus animo secum. cui fidus Achates

it comes et paribus curis vestigia figit.

160 multa inter sese vario sermone serebant,

quem socium exanimem vates, quod corpus humandum

diceret. atque illi Misenum in litore sicco,

ut venere, vident indigna morte peremptum,

Misenum Aeoliden, quo non praestantior alter

aere ciere viros Martemque accendere cantu.

Hectoris hic magni fuerat comes, Hectora circum

et lituo pugnas insignis obibat et hasta.

postquam illum vita victor spoliavit Achilles,

Dardanio Aeneae sese fortissimus heros

170 addiderat socium, non inferiora secutus.

sed tum, forte cava dum personat aequora concha,

The whole fleet. Carry this man to a right
Resting place, lay him into his tomb,
210   Sacrifice herds of black sheep as your first
Votive offerings. Then and then only
Will you view the forests of Styx, those realms
Barred to the living." She said these things,
Pressed her lips shut and went silent.

Aeneas, his face sadder now, looking downcast,
Walked away from the cave, not sure what to think
Or expect. Trusty Achates walked at his side,
In step with his friend, apprehensive,
Intense, the give and take of their talk
220   Uncertain yet urgent: who, for example, might be
The dead comrade the Sibyl enjoined them
To bury? And then they saw him, Misenus,
On a dry stretch of beach—they came up and saw
The son of Aeolus, unfairly, peremptorily
Called to his death, this man unsurpassed
At rallying fighters, blaring the war call
On his bronze trumpet. Once he had been
Great Hector's comrade, standing by him in battle,
Unmistakable, known by his trumpet and spear.
230   Then after Achilles had savaged Hector to death
This staunchest of heroes, unwilling to join
A less worthy cause, chose to follow Aeneas.
But a mad moment came when the trumpeter blew
Resonant notes from a conch shell over the waves,

demens, et cantu vocat in certamina divos,
aemulus exceptum Triton, si credere dignum est,
inter saxa virum spumosa immerserat unda.
ergo omnes magno circum clamore fremebant,
praecipue pius Aeneas. tum iussa Sibyllae,
haud mora, festinant flentes aramque sepulcri
congerere arboribus caeloque educere certant.
itur in antiquam silvam, stabula alta ferarum;
180   procumbunt piceae, sonat icta securibus ilex
fraxineaeque trabes cuneis et fissile robur
scinditur, advolvunt ingentis montibus ornos.
      Nec non Aeneas opera inter talia primus
hortatur socios paribusque accingitur armis.
atque haec ipse suo tristi cum corde volutat,
aspectans silvam immensam, et sic forte precatur:
"si nunc se nobis ille aureus arbore ramus
ostendat nemore in tanto! quando omnia vere
heu nimium de te vates, Misene, locuta est."
190   vix ea fatus erat, geminae cum forte columbae
ipsa sub ora viri caelo venere volantes
et viridi sedere solo. tum maximus heros

Intending to challenge the gods
To a musical contest. Triton was shaken
With envy (hard as it is to believe) and surged up
And drowned him in a sudden backwash of foam.

So the Trojans assembled and lifted their voices
240   In mourning, none louder, more devout than Aeneas;
Then, still in tears, they set to at once, eager
To follow the Sibyl's instruction, piling up logs,
Building an altar-pyre that rose toward the heavens.
High in the virgin forest, near dens of wild beasts,
Holm oaks echo the crack of their axes, spruce trees
Get felled, they hammer in wedges, split open
Beams of the ash and the tougher cross-grain of oak.
Big rowan trees crash and roll from the hilltop down.

As all this proceeded, Aeneas was to the fore,
250   Geared out like the rest, cheering everyone on.
But he kept gazing up at that high stretch of forest,
Sadly preoccupied, pondering things in his heart
Until a prayer rose to his lips and he said:
"If only that golden bough would show itself
On its tree in the deep forest den—for everything
The prophetess said about you, Misenus, was true,
Altogether too true!" And almost immediately
A pair of doves chanced down from the sky
In full view, and settled on the green grass;
260   In them the great hero knew his own mother's birds

maternas agnovit aves laetusque precatur:
"este duces o, si qua via est, cursumque per auras
derigite in lucos, ubi pinguem dives opacat
ramus humum. tuque o, dubiis ne defice rebus,
diva parens." sic effatus vestigia pressit,
observans, quae signa ferant, quo tendere pergant.
pascentes illae tantum prodire volando,
200   quantum acie possent oculi servare sequentum.
inde ubi venere ad fauces grave olentis Averni,
tollunt se celeres liquidumque per aëra lapsae
sedibus optatis geminae super arbore sidunt,
discolor unde auri per ramos aura refulsit.
quale solet silvis brumali frigore viscum
fronde virere nova, quod non sua seminat arbos,
et croceo fetu teretis circumdare truncos:
talis erat species auri frondentis opaca
ilice, sic leni crepitabat brattea vento.
210   corripit Aeneas extemplo avidusque refringit
cunctantem, et vatis portat sub tecta Sibyllae.

Nec minus interea Misenum in litore Teucri
flebant, et cineri ingrato suprema ferebant.
principio pinguem taedis et robore secto

And prayed and rejoiced: "O, if a way can be found.
Be you my guides. Hold course through the air,
Lead on to the grove where that opulent bough
Overshadows the rich forest floor. And you,
O my goddess mother, do not abandon me
In this time of confusion." With that he halted
To watch for what signs they might give, what place
They might make for. But the doves kept on going,
Now feeding, now flying ahead, at all times
270   Staying in view of the eyes that pursued them.

Then when they came to the fuming gorge at Avernus
They swept up through clear air and back down
To their chosen perch, a tree that was two trees
In one, green-leafed yet refulgent with gold.
Like mistletoe shining in cold winter woods,
Gripping its tree but not grafted, always in leaf,
Its yellowy berries in sprays curled round the bole—
Those flickering gold tendrils lit up the dark
Overhang of the oak and chimed in the breeze.
280   There and then Aeneas took hold of the bough
And although it resisted greedily tore it off,
Then carried it back to the Sibyl's cavern.

On the beach the Trojans were mourning
Misenus as sorely as ever, paying
Their last respects to the inert ash.
With resinous pinewood and cut-off sections of oak

ingentem struxere pyram, cui frondibus atris
intexunt latera, et feralis ante cupressos
constituunt, decorantque super fulgentibus armis.
pars calidos latices et aëna undantia flammis
expediunt, corpusque lavant frigentis et ungunt.
220   fit gemitus. tum membra toro defleta reponunt
purpureasque super vestes, velamina nota,
coniciunt. pars ingenti subiere feretro,
triste ministerium, et subiectam more parentum
aversi tenuere facem. congesta cremantur
turea dona, dapes, fuso crateres olivo.
postquam conlapsi cineres et flamma quievit,
reliquias vino et bibulam lavere favillam,
ossaque lecta cado texit Corynaeus aëno.
idem ter socios pura circumtulit unda,
230   spargens rore levi et ramo felicis olivae,
lustravitque viros, dixitque novissima verba.
at pius Aeneas ingenti mole sepulcrum
imponit, suaque arma viro remumque tubamque,
monte sub aërio, qui nunc Misenus ab illo
dicitur, aeternumque tenet per saecula nomen.
        His actis propere exsequitur praecepta Sibyllae.

They constructed first a huge pyre, dressing its flanks
With branches darkly in leaf, fencing the base
With funereal cypress, crowning all
290   With resplendent armour and weapons. Some heated
Water in bubbling vats above open fires, washed
And anointed the corpse, then raised the lament.
Next, when the weeping was over, they laid him out
On the ritual couch, his remains swathed in purple,
Familiar robes of the dead. Some stepped in
To lift high the great bier—a grievous observance—
And with eyes averted, as ancestral custom required,
Touched a blazing torch to the base of the pyre.
Gifts of food, piled offerings, incense, and bowls
300   Brimming over with oil went up in the flames.
Then when the fire had died, collapsing to ash,
They poured wine on his parched dust; and Corynaeus
Collected the bones in a bronze urn and sealed them.
Three times he moved round the company, sprinkling
Clean water for purification, asperging men lightly
From an olive branch, dewy with promise; then gave
The farewell. And under a high airy hill
Aeneas reared a magnificent tomb
Hung with the dead man's equipment, his oar
310   And his trumpet, so the hill is now called
Misenus, a name that will live down the ages.

Once this was done, Aeneas quickly proceeded
To follow the Sibyl's instructions. There was a cave,

spelunca alta fuit vastoque immanis hiatu,

scrupea, tuta lacu nigro nemorumque tenebris,

quam super haud ullae poterant impune volantes

240 tendere iter pinnis: talis sese halitus atris

faucibus effundens supera ad convexa ferebat

unde locum Grai dixerunt nomine Aornum.

quattuor hic primum nigrantis terga iuvencos

constituit, frontique invergit vina sacerdos,

et summas carpens media inter cornua saetas

ignibus imponit sacris, libamina prima,

voce vocans Hecaten caeloque Ereboque potentem.

supponunt alii cultros tepidumque cruorem

succipiunt pateris. ipse atri velleris agnam

250 Aeneas matri Eumenidum magnaeque sorori

ense ferit sterilemque tibi, Proserpina, vaccam.

tum Stygio regi nocturnas incohat aras

et solida imponit taurorum viscera flammis,

pingue super oleum fundens ardentibus extis.

ecce autem primi sub lumina solis et ortus

sub pedibus mugire solum et iuga coepta moveri

silvarum, visaeque canes ululare per umbram

A deep rough-walled cleft, stone jaws agape
Above a dark lake, with the lake and a grove
For protection and shelter. No creature of air
Could wing its way safely over that water,
Such were the noxious fumes spewing up
From the murky chasm into the vault of the heavens.
320 (The Greeks therefore called it Avernus, "place
Without birds.")
                    The first thing the priestess did here
Was line up four black heifers, pour libations of wine
On their foreheads, clip off the bristles that sprouted
Between their horns and commence sacrifice,
Offering them on the flames, all the while praying
Her clamorous prayers to Hecate, she who has power
Under the earth and above it. Others draw blades,
Catching warm blood in vessels. Aeneas himself
330 With a stroke of his sword, to honour Dark Night
And her sister, the Earth, slays a black-fleeced lamb,
And to honour you, Proserpina, a heifer,
Infertile. Then for the King of the Underworld
He illumines the dark, consecrating an altar
Where he burns whole carcasses and pours
Sluggish oil on the glowing entrails of bulls.
But all of a sudden, between the first glimmer
And full rise of the sun, the ground at their feet
Starts rumbling and shaking, the wooded heights
340 Are atremble, and in the uncanny light what they hear
Sounds like the howling of dogs as Hecate approaches.

27

adventante dea. "procul o, procul este, profani,"
conclamat vates, "totoque absistite luco;
260   tuque invade viam vaginaque eripe ferrum:
nunc animis opus, Aenea, nunc pectore firmo."
tantum effata furens antro se immisit aperto;
ille ducem haud timidis vadentem passibus aequat.

       Di, quibus imperium est animarum, umbraeque silentes
et Chaos et Phlegethon, loca nocte tacentia late,
sit mihi fas audita loqui; sit numine vestro
pandere res alta terra et caligine mersas.

       Ibant obscuri sola sub nocte per umbram
perque domos Ditis vacuas et inania regna,
270   quale per incertam lunam sub luce maligna
est iter in silvis, ubi caelum condidit umbra
Iuppiter, et rebus nox abstulit atra colorem.
vestibulum ante ipsum primisque in faucibus Orci
Luctus et ultrices posuere cubilia Curae,
pallentesque habitant Morbi tristisque Senectus

"Out from here," the seeress is shouting, "out,
Anyone here not initiate—all such,
Depart from the grove. But not you, Aeneas:
Take you the sword from your scabbard, go ahead
On the road. Now will spirit be tested,
Now, now your courage must hold." So saying, rapt
And unstoppable, she hurled herself into the mouth
Of the wide-open cave, and he, without fear,
350   Kept in step as she guided him forward.

Gods who rule over souls! Shades who subsist
In the silence! Chaos and Phlegethon, O you hushed
Nocturnal expanses, let assent be forthcoming
As I tell what's been given to tell, let assent be divine
As I unveil things profoundly beyond us,
Mysteries and truths buried under the earth.

On they went then in darkness, through the lonely
Shadowing night, a nowhere of deserted dwellings,
Dim phantasmal reaches where Pluto is king—
360   Like following a forest path by the hovering light
Of a moon that clouds and unclouds at Jupiter's whim,
While the colours of the world pall in the gloom.

In front of the house of the dead,
Between its dread jambs, is a courtyard where pain
And self-wounding thoughts have ensconced themelves.
Here too are pallid diseases, the sorrows of age,

et Metus et malesuada Fames ac turpis Egestas,
terribiles visu formae, Letumque Labosque:
tum consanguineus Leti Sopor et mala mentis
Gaudia, mortiferumque adverso in limine Bellum
280 ferreique Eumenidum thalami et Discordia demens,
vipereum crinem vittis innexa cruentis.
     In medio ramos annosaque bracchia pandit
ulmus opaca, ingens, quam sedem Somnia vulgo
vana tenere ferunt, foliisque sub omnibus haerent.
multaque praeterea variarum monstra ferarum,
Centauri in foribus stabulant Scyllaeque biformes
et centumgeminus Briareus ac belua Lernae,
horrendum stridens, flammisque armata Chimaera,
Gorgones Harpyiaeque et forma tricorporis umbrae.
290 corripit hic subita trepidus formidine ferrum
Aeneas, strictamque aciem venientibus offert;
et, ni docta comes tenuis sine corpore vitas
admoneat volitare cava sub imagine formae,
inruat et frustra ferro diverberet umbras.
     Hinc via, Tartarei quae fert Acherontis ad undas.
turbidus hic caeno vastaque voragine gurges

Hunger that drives men to crime, agonies of the mind,
Poverty that demeans—all of these haunting nightmares
Have their beds in the niches. Death too, and sleep,
370 The brother of death, and terror, and guilty pleasures
That memory battens on. Also close by that doorway:
The iron cells of the Furies, death-dealing War
And fanatical Violence, her viper-tresses astream
In a bloodstained tangle of ribbons.
                                       Right in the middle
Stands an elm, copious, darkly aflutter, old branches
Spread wide like arms, and here, it is said,
False dreams come to roost, clinging together
On the undersides of the leaves. At the gates,
380 Monstrosities brood in their pens, bewildering beasts
Of every form and description: two-natured Centaurs
And Scyllas, hundred-headed Briareus, the beast of Lerna,
Loathsome and hissing, and fire-fanged Chimaera;
Gorgons and Harpies too, and the looming menace
Of triple-framed Geryon. Faced with this rout,
Aeneas is thrown into panic, pulls out his sword,
Swings it round in defence, and had not his guide
In her wisdom forewarned him
That these were lives without substance, phantoms,
390 Apparitional forms, he would have charged
And tried to draw blood from shadows.

A road starts here that leads to Acheron river.
Here too is the roiling abyss, heaving with mud,

aestuat, atque omnem Cocyto eructat harenam.
portitor has horrendus aquas et flumina servat
terribili squalore Charon, cui plurima mento
300   canities inculta iacet, stant lumina flamma,
sordidus ex umeris nodo dependet amictus.
ipse ratem conto subigit velisque ministrat
et ferruginea subvectat corpora cumba,
iam senior, sed cruda deo viridisque senectus.
huc omnis turba ad ripas effusa ruebat,
matres atque viri, defunctaque corpora vita
magnanimum heroum, pueri innuptaeque puellae
impositique rogis iuvenes ante ora parentum:
quam multa in silvis autumni frigore primo
310   lapsa cadunt folia, aut ad terram gurgite ab alto
quam multae glomerantur aves, ubi frigidus annus
trans pontum fugat et terris immittit apricis.
stabant orantes primi transmittere cursum
tendebantque manus ripae ulterioris amore.
navita sed tristis nunc hos nunc accipit illos,
ast alios longe submotos arcet harena.

      Aeneas miratus enim motusque tumultu
"dic," ait, "o virgo, quid vult concursus ad amnem?

Venting a silty upsurge into Cocytus,
And beside these flowing streams and flooded wastes
A ferryman keeps watch, surly, filthy and bedraggled
Charon. His chin is bearded with unclean white shag;
The eyes stand in his head and glow; a grimy cloak
Flaps out from a knot tied at the shoulder.
400   All by himself he poles the boat, hoists sail
And ferries dead souls in his rusted craft,
Old but still a god, and in a god old age
Is green and hardy.
                              Hereabouts a crowd
Came pouring to the banks, women and men,
And noble-minded heroes separated now
From their living flesh, young boys, unmarried girls,
And sons cremated before their fathers' eyes:
Continuous as the streaming leaves nipped off
410   By first frost in the autumn woods, or flocks of birds
Blown inland from the stormy ocean, when the year
Turns cold and drives them to migrate
To countries in the sun. There they stood, those souls,
Begging to be the first allowed across, stretching out
Arms that hankered towards the farther shore.
The stern boatman permits one group to board
And now another, but the rest he denies passage,
Driving them back, away from the sandy banks.

Amazed and then moved by all this press and pleading,
420   Aeneas asks his guide: "What does it mean, O Sibyl,

quidve petunt animae? vel quo discrimine ripas

320 hae linquunt, illae remis vada livida verrunt?"

olli sic breviter fata est longaeva sacerdos:

"Anchisa generate, deum certissima proles,

Cocyti stagna alta vides Stygiamque paludem,

di cuius iurare timent et fallere numen.

haec omnis, quam cernis, inops inhumataque turba est;

portitor ille Charon; hi, quos vehit unda, sepulti;

nec ripas datur horrendas et rauca fluenta

transportare prius quam sedibus ossa quierunt.

centum errant annos volitantque haec litora circum;

330 tum demum admissi stagna exoptata revisunt."

constitit Anchisa satus et vestigia pressit,

multa putans sortemque animo miseratus iniquam.

cernit ibi maestos et mortis honore carentis

Leucaspim et Lyciae ductorem classis Oronten,

quos simul a Troia ventosa per aequora vectos

obruit Auster, aqua involvens navemque virosque.

Ecce gubernator sese Palinurus agebat,

This push to the riverbank? What do these souls desire?
What decides that one group is held back, another
Rowed across the muddy waters?"

                                            "Son of Anchises,"
The venerable one replied, "O true born son of heaven,
What you see here are the standing pools
Of Cocytus and the Stygian marsh.
These are the names invoked when gods swear oaths
They will never dare to break. That crowd in front of you
430   Died but were left unburied, with no help or hope.
The ferryman is Charon. The ones on board his craft
Are the buried. Not until bones have found a last
Resting place will shades be let across
These gurgling currents, their doom instead to wander
And haunt about the banks for a hundred years.
Then and then only are they again allowed
To approach the brink and waters that they long for."

Aeneas stopped and stood there, lost in thought,
Comprehending, pity in his heart
440   At their misfortune, then caught sight of Leucaspis
And Orontes, who'd captained the Lycian fleet,
Downcast men, denied the rites of the dead:
On their journey out from Troy, a southern gale
Struck ship and crew in heavy seas, and both
Were swept away, overwhelmed in the turmoil.

And now there appears his helmsman, Palinurus,
Who not long since had pitched and tumbled off

qui Libyco nuper cursu, dum sidera servat,

exciderat puppi mediis effusus in undis.

340 hunc ubi vix multa maestum cognovit in umbra,

sic prior adloquitur: "quis te, Palinure, deorum

eripuit nobis medioque sub aequore mersit?

dic age. namque mihi, fallax haud ante repertus,

hoc uno responso animum delusit Apollo,

qui fore te ponto incolumem finisque canebat

venturum Ausonios. en haec promissa fides est?"

ille autem: "neque te Phoebi cortina fefellit,

dux Anchisiade, nec me deus aequore mersit.

namque gubernaclum multa vi forte revulsum,

350 cui datus haerebam custos cursusque regebam,

praecipitans traxi mecum. maria aspera iuro

non ullum pro me tantum cepisse timorem,

quam tua ne, spoliata armis, excussa magistro,

deficeret tantis navis surgentibus undis.

tris Notus hibernas immensa per aequora noctes

vexit me violentus aqua; vix lumine quarto

prospexi Italiam summa sublimis ab unda.

The stern into open sea, as he held course
From Africa, eyes fixed upon the stars.

450 To whom Aeneas, once he recognised
His sad form in the congregating dark,
Spoke first: "Which god snatched you from us,
Palinurus, and drowned you in the deep?
Tell, O tell what happened. Never until now
Did Apollo's oracle prove false, but this time
He deceived me: you would survive the waves,
He prophesied, and land safe on the shore
Of Italia. Is this how he keeps his word?"
But Palinurus answered, "My captain, son

460 Of Anchises, the god Apollo's oracle
Did not play you false, nor did any god
Plunge me into the waves. What happened was this:
The steering oar I held and was in charge of
Snapped in a sudden gale and as I fell
I dragged it down with me. But I swear by Ocean
The fear I had for myself then was as nothing
To the fear I had for your ship.
Stripped of her tackle, her steersman overboard,
Would she not wallow and founder

470 In those mountainous seas? For three nights,
Through horizonless surge, a south wind
Hurled me and burled me. The fourth day at dawn,
I rose on a swell and got my first glimpse
Of Italia. Little by little then I was making headway,
Slugging towards land in my waterlogged clothes,

paulatim adnabam terrae; iam tuta tenebam,

ni gens crudelis madida cum veste gravatum,

360 prensantemque uncis manibus capita aspera montis,

ferro invasisset praedamque ignara putasset.

nunc me fluctus habet versantque in litore venti.

quod te per caeli iucundum lumen et auras,

per genitorem oro, per spes surgentis Iuli,

eripe me his, invicte, malis: aut tu mihi terram

inice (namque potes) portusque require Velinos;

aut tu, si qua via est, si quam tibi diva creatrix

ostendit (neque enim, credo, sine numine divum

flumina tanta paras Stygiamque innare paludem),

370 da dextram misero et tecum me tolle per undas,

sedibus ut saltem placidis in morte quiescam."

    Talia fatus erat, coepit cum talia vates:

"unde haec, o Palinure, tibi tam dira cupido?

tu Stygias inhumatus aquas amnemque severum

Eumenidum aspicies ripamve iniussus adibis?

desine fata deum flecti sperare precando.

Getting a grip on the razor-backed ridges,

When savage locals appeared with drawn swords,

A pack who for want of knowing assumed

That I'd be rich pickings. Now surf keeps me dandled,

480   The shore winds loll me and roll me.

"You, therefore, you the unbowed, the unbroken,

I implore, by the cheerful light of the sky

And its breezes, by your father and your hopes

As the father of Iulus, get me away

From this place, put an end to my woes.

Either scatter the handful of earth

On my corpse, which you easily can

Once you're back in the harbour at Velia,

Or else—if there be a way, if your goddess-mother

490   Can direct you to one—for I believe you are bound

To enjoy the favour of heaven, prepared as you are

To face these vast waterways and set sail

On the Stygian marsh—reach out your hand

To one who is suffering, take me with you

Over the waves, so that in death at the least

I shall find a calm haven."

                    That was his plea

To Aeneas, and this was the answer he got

From the Sibyl: "What madness is this, Palinurus?

500   You who aren't even buried, what makes you think

You can look on the waters of Styx or the Furies'

Grim river? You have not been called to the bank.

Banish the thought that praying can ever affect

sed cape dicta memor, duri solacia casus:

nam tua finitimi, longe lateque per urbes

prodigiis acti caelestibus, ossa piabunt

380   et statuent tumulum et tumulo sollemnia mittent,

aeternumque locus Palinuri nomen habebit."

his dictis curae emotae, pulsusque parumper

corde dolor tristi; gaudet cognomine terra.

        Ergo iter inceptum peragunt fluvioque propinquant.

navita quos iam inde ut Stygia prospexit ab unda

per tacitum nemus ire pedemque advertere ripae,

sic prior adgreditur dictis atque increpat ultro:

"quisquis es, armatus qui nostra ad flumina tendis,

fare age, quid venias, iam istinc, et comprime gressum.

390   umbrarum hic locus est, Somni Noctisque soporae;

corpora viva nefas Stygia vectare carina.

nec vero Alciden me sum laetatus euntem

accepisse lacu nec Thesea Pirithoumque,

dis quamquam geniti atque invicti viribus essent.

Tartareum ille manu custodem in vincla petivit,

The edicts of gods. Your plight is a hard one,
But hear and remember my words: they should be
A comfort. What will happen is this:
Your bones will be reverenced; the sky
Will reveal signs and portents, in cities
On every side populations will know
510 To build you a tomb and observe solemn custom
With offerings year after year. And the place
For all time will bear the name Palinurus."
These words lifted his heart and raised,
For a moment, his spirits. The thought
Of the land in his name makes him happy.

So now they resumed their journey and kept going
Until they were near the river, moving through
Silent woodland towards the bank, when Charon
From his boat out on the water spied them
520 And began to remonstrate, on the attack
Before they even spoke: "You, whoever you are,
Approaching our river under arms, stop there,
Not one step farther, and say what brings you:
This is the country of the shades, of heavy-lidded
Night and sleep. It is a thing forbidden
To load the Stygian ferry with living bodies.
I rue the day I carried Hercules
And Theseus and Pirithous, sons of gods as they were,
Strongmen, invincibles. Hercules arrived
530 To chain up and restrain the hellmouth watchdog,

ipsius a solio regis, traxitque trementem;

hi dominam Ditis thalamo deducere adorti."

quae contra breviter fata est Amphrysia vates:

"nullae hic insidiae tales (absiste moveri),

400   nec vim tela ferunt; licet ingens ianitor antro

aeternum latrans exsanguis terreat umbras;

casta licet patrui servet Proserpina limen.

Troïus Aeneas, pietate insignis et armis,

ad genitorem imas Erebi descendit ad umbras.

si te nulla movet tantae pietatis imago,

at ramum hunc" (aperit ramum, qui veste latebat)

"agnoscas." tumida ex ira tum corda residunt.

nec plura his. ille admirans venerabile donum

fatalis virgae, longo post tempore visum,

410   caeruleam advertit puppim ripaeque propinquat.

inde alias animas, quae per iuga longa sedebant,

deturbat laxatque foros; simul accipit alveo

ingentem Aeneam. gemuit sub pondere cumba

sutilis et multam accepit rimosa paludem.

tandem trans fluvium incolumis vatemque virumque

informi limo glaucaque exponit in ulva.

To steal him from the very throne of the king—
And did carry the panicked beast away. The others
Tried to abduct the queen from Pluto's bed."
To which the soothsaying priestess made reply:
"Nothing like that is being plotted here. These arms
And weapons present you with no threat, so be calm.
Let the monster cave-dog howl his howl forever
And keep on terrifying bloodless shades,
Proserpina be her pure self behind her uncle's doors.
540   Aeneas of Troy, renowned for his right life
And warrior prowess, descends among the shades,
Down to death's deepest regions, to see his father.
If the sight of such devotedness won't move you,
You nevertheless must recognise this bough,"
And she shows the bough concealed by her cloak.
Charon quietens then, his bad temper subsides,
He says no more. It is long since he beheld
The holy proffer of that fateful branch. He turns
His dark barge round and steers for the shore.
550   Other souls ensconced on the long thwarts
He hurries off up gangways, then at once
Hands mighty Aeneas down into the vessel.
Under that weight the boat's plied timbers groan
And thick marsh water oozes through the leaks,
But in the end it is a safe crossing, and he lands
Soldier and soothsayer on slithery mud, knee-deep
In grey-green sedge.
                              Here Cerberus keeps watch,

Cerberus haec ingens latratu regna trifauci
personat, adverso recubans immanis in antro.
cui vates, horrere videns iam colla colubris,
420   melle soporatam et medicatis frugibus offam
obicit. ille fame rabida tria guttura pandens
corripit obiectam, atque immania terga resolvit
fusus humi totoque ingens extenditur antro.
occupat Aeneas aditum custode sepulto
evaditque celer ripam inremeabilis undae.
      Continuo auditae voces vagitus et ingens
infantumque animae flentes, in limine primo
quos dulcis vitae exsortis et ab ubere raptos
abstulit atra dies et funere mersit acerbo.
430   hos iuxta falso damnati crimine mortis.
nec vero hae sine sorte datae, sine iudice, sedes:
quaesitor Minos urnam movet; ille silentum
consiliumque vocat, vitasque et crimina discit.
proxima deinde tenent maesti loca, qui sibi letum
insontes peperere manu lucemque perosi
proiecere animas. quam vellent aethere in alto

Growling from three gullets, his brute bulk couched
560   In the cave, facing down all comers. But the Sibyl,
Seeing snake-hackles bristle on his necks,
Flings him a dumpling of soporific honey
And heavily drugged grain. The ravenous triple maw
Yawns open, snaffles the sop it has been thrown
Until next thing the enormous flanks go slack
And the inert form slumps to the cave floor.
Thus, with the watchdog sunk in a deep sleep,
Aeneas gains entry and is quick to put behind him
The bank of that river none comes back across.

570   At once a sound of crying fills the air, the high wails
And weeping of infant souls, little ones denied
Their share of sweet life, torn from the breast
On life's very doorstep. A dark day bore them off
And sank them in untimely death. Next to them
Are those condemned to death on false charges,
Although here they are assigned their proper verdicts
By a rightly chosen jury. Minos, the judge,
Presides and shakes the urn, convenes a panel
Of the silent dead, seeking to establish
580   Men's characters and crimes. Farther on
Is the dwelling place of those unhappy spirits
Who died by their own hand, simply driven
By life to a fierce rejection of the light.
How they long now for the open air above,
How willingly they would endure the lot

nunc et pauperiem et duros perferre labores!
fas obstat tristisque palus inamabilis undae
alligat et noviens Styx interfusa coercet.

440   Nec procul hinc partem fusi monstrantur in omnem
Lugentes Campi; sic illos nomine dicunt.
hic, quos durus amor crudeli tabe peredit,
secreti celant calles et myrtea circum
silva tegit; curae non ipsa in morte relinquunt.
his Phaedram Procrinque locis maestamque Eriphylen,
crudelis nati monstrantem vulnera, cernit,
Euadnenque et Pasiphaën; his Laodamia
it comes et iuvenis quondam, nunc femina, Caeneus
rursus et in veterem fato revoluta figuram.

450 inter quas Phoenissa recens a vulnere Dido
errabat silva in magna. quam Troïus heros
ut primum iuxta stetit agnovitque per umbras
obscuram, qualem primo qui surgere mense
aut videt aut vidisse putat per nubila lunam,
demisit lacrimas dulcique adfatus amore est:

Of exhausted workers and the hard-wrought poor.
But their way is barred by laws of gods. The waste
And desolate marsh water laps round,
River Styx with its nine loops binds and bounds them.

590 Not far from here the fields called the Fields
Of Mourning stretch out in all directions.
On these plains, hidden on shadowy paths,
Secluded and embowered in myrtle groves,
Are those who suffered hard and cruel decline
In thrall to an unremitting love. Their griefs
Do not relent, not even in death. Here Aeneas saw
Among other lovers Phaedra and Procris,
And sad Eriphyle, pointing to the wounds
Dealt by her callous son. Evadne too,
600 And Pasiphaë. And moving in step with them
Laodamia, and Caeneus who in her time had known
Life as a man, though fate had now restored
The figure of the woman she once was.

Along with these, still nursing her raw wound,
Dido of Carthage strayed in the great forest.
As soon as the Trojan came close and made out
Her dimly wavering form among the shadows,
He was like one who sees or imagines he has seen
A new moon rising up among the clouds
610 On the first day of the month; there and then
He wept and spoke these loving, tender words:

"infelix Dido, verus mihi nuntius ergo
venerat exstinctam, ferroque extrema secutam?
funeris heu! tibi causa fui? per sidera iuro,
per superos, et si qua fides tellure sub ima est,
460   invitus, regina, tuo de litore cessi.
sed me iussa deum, quae nunc has ire per umbras,
per loca senta situ cogunt noctemque profundam,
imperiis egere suis; nec credere quivi
hunc tantum tibi me discessu ferre dolorem.
siste gradum teque aspectu ne subtrahe nostro.
quem fugis? extremum fato, quod te adloquor, hoc est."
talibus Aeneas ardentem et torva tuentem
lenibat dictis animum lacrimasque ciebat.
illa solo fixos oculos aversa tenebat
470   nec magis incepto vultum sermone movetur,
quam si dura silex aut stet Marpesia cautes.
tandem corripuit sese atque inimica refugit
in nemus umbriferum, coniunx ubi pristinus illi
respondet curis aequatque Sychaeus amorem.
nec minus Aeneas, casu percussus iniquo,

"Unhappy Dido! So the news I got was true,
That you had left the world, had taken a sword
And bade your last farewell. Was I, O was I to blame
For your death? I swear by the stars, by the powers
Above and by any truth there may be under earth,
I embarked from your shore, my queen, unwillingly.
Orders from the gods, which compel me now
To travel among shades in this mouldering world,
620   This bottomless pit of night, dictated
Obedience then as well. How could I believe
My going would devastate you with such grief?
Stay a moment, don't slip out of our sight.
Is there someone you are trying to avoid?
These words I'm saying to you are the last
Fate will permit me, ever."

                    Pleading like this,
Tears welling up inside him, Aeneas tried
To placate her fiery spirit and soften
630   Her fierce gaze; but she, averting her face,
Her eyes fixed steadily on the ground, turned
And showed no sign of having heard, no more
Than if her features had been carved in flint
Or Parian marble. At length she swept away
And fled, implacable, into the dappling shadows
Of the grove, where Sychaeus, her husband
In another earlier time, feels for her pain
And reciprocates the love she bears him still;
While Aeneas, no less stricken by the injustice

prosequitur lacrimis longe et miseratur euntem.

      Inde datum molitur iter. iamque arva tenebant
ultima, quae bello clari secreta frequentant.
hic illi occurrit Tydeus, hic inclutus armis
480   Parthenopaeus et Adrasti pallentis imago.
hic multum fleti ad superos belloque caduci
Dardanidae, quos ille omnis longo ordine cernens
ingemuit, Glaucumque Medontaque Thersilochumque,
tris Antenoridas, Cererique sacrum Polyboeten,
Idaeumque etiam currus, etiam arma tenentem.
circumstant animae dextra laevaque frequentes.
nec vidisse semel satis est; iuvat usque morari
et conferre gradum et veniendi discere causas.
at Danaum proceres Agamemnoniaeque phalanges,
490   ut videre virum fulgentiaque arma per umbras,
ingenti trepidare metu: pars vertere terga,
ceu quondam petiere rates; pars tollere vocem
exiguam, inceptus clamor frustratur hiantis.

      Atque hic Priamiden laniatum corpore toto
Deiphobum videt et lacerum crudeliter ora,

Of her fate, gazes into the distance after her,
Gazes through tears, and pities her as she goes.

Then he braces himself for the journey still to come
And soon they arrive in the farthest outlying fields,
The hosting grounds of those renowned in war.
In one place Tydeus meets him, in another
Parthenopaeus, glorious in arms, and the bloodless
Shade of Adrastus; elsewhere the Trojan chieftains
Who fell in battle, much mourned in the world above.
And now he also moaned to see them
650 Thronging in such numbers: Glaucus, Medon
And Thersilochus, Antenor's three sons; Polyboetes,
The priest of Ceres; and Idaeus, still
The chariot driver, still dressed in his armour.
From right and left souls crowd and jostle close,
Eager for more than just a look at him; they want
His company, the joy of keeping in step, talking,
Learning why he has come. But the Greek captains
And the gleaming cohorts once led by Agamemnon
Cowered in panic when they saw Aeneas
660 Advance in dazzling armour through the gloom.
Some turned to flee as they had once to the ships,
Some raised a spectral cry that came to nothing,
Dying away as it left their gaping mouths.

And here Aeneas caught sight of Priam's son,
Deiphobus, mutilated in every part, his face

ora manusque ambas, populataque tempora raptis

auribus et truncas inhonesto vulnere naris.

vix adeo agnovit pavitantem ac dira tegentem

supplicia, et notis compellat vocibus ultro:

500   "Deiphobe armipotens, genus alto a sanguine Teucri,

quis tam crudelis optavit sumere poenas?

cui tantum de te licuit? mihi fama suprema

nocte tulit fessum vasta te caede Pelasgum

procubuisse super confusae stragis acervum.

tunc egomet tumulum Rhoeteo litore inanem

constitui et magna Manis ter voce vocavi.

nomen et arma locum servant; te, amice, nequivi

conspicere et patria decedens ponere terra."

ad quae Priamides: "nihil o tibi, amice, relictum;

510   omnia Deiphobo solvisti et funeris umbris.

sed me fata mea et scelus exitiale Lacaenae

his mersere malis; illa haec monumenta reliquit.

namque ut supremam falsa inter gaudia noctem

In shreds—his face and his two hands—
Ears torn from his head, and his nostrils
(A low dishonourable wounding, this)
His nostrils cut away: unrecognisable almost
670   As he shivered and shrank into himself to hide
The cruel laceration. Aeneas,
In a voice well known to him, spoke first, resolutely:
"Deiphobus, mightiest in the field, offspring
Of Teucer's ancient line, who was there capable
Of such mutilation? Who let themselves
Run so ruthlessly amok? The story I heard was this:
On the last night in Troy, you waded in Greek blood
Till you fell exhausted, fell like a dead man
On a heap of their slobbered corpses. That is why
680   I raised an empty tomb for you at Rhoetum,
On the shore, and with my three loud cries
Invoked your spirit. Your name now and your arms
Hallow that spot. But not you in the flesh, my friend,
Whom I could neither see as I embarked
Nor bury in home ground."
                     Priam's son replied:
"And you, my friend, you left no thing undone.
You paid the right attention to Deiphobus,
Dead man and shade. It was my destiny
690   And the criminal, widowing schemes of my lady
Of Sparta wrecked and ruined me. What you see
Are the love bites she left me in remembrance
Of that last night, of all our city's nights

egerimus, nosti; et nimium meminisse necesse est.

cum fatalis equus saltu super ardua venit

Pergama et armatum peditem gravis attulit alvo,

illa, chorum simulans, euhantis orgia circum

ducebat Phrygias; flammam media ipsa tenebat

ingentem et summa Danaos ex arce vocabat.

520 tum me, confectum curis somnoque gravatum,

infelix habuit thalamus, pressitque iacentem

dulcis et alta quies placidaeque simillima morti.

egregia interea coniunx arma omnia tectis

emovet, et fidum capiti subduxerat ensem;

intra tecta vocat Menelaum et limina pandit,

scilicet id magnum sperans fore munus amanti,

et famam exstingui veterum sic posse malorum.

quid moror? inrumpunt thalamo, comes additus una

hortator scelerum Aeolides. di, talia Grais

530 instaurate, pio si poenas ore reposco.

sed te qui vivum casus, age fare vicissim,

attulerint. pelagine venis erroribus actus

an monitu divum? aut quae te fortuna fatigat,

ut tristis sine sole domos, loca turbida, adires?”

The most jubilant and most deluded. But this you know
Too well already, for how could you forget?
When the horse that was our fate came at a leap
On to the heights of Troy, big in the belly
With armed men, she was to the fore, involved
In the dance, contriving to lead our women
700   In the loud frenzy of the bacchanal.
Up she went to our citadel, in her hand
A torch conspicuously ablaze,
Signalling to the Greeks. And me then! Me
In my god-cursed marriage-bed, lying dead beat,
Far gone, giving in to sleep, sweet, welcoming,
Drowsy sleep, serene almost as death. Meanwhile,
My paragon of a bride had cleared the house
Of every weapon and even stolen the sword
From underneath my head; and now she opened doors
710   And called for Menelaus to come in, hoping, no doubt,
That this grand favour to her lover boy
Would blot out memories of old betrayals.
But why say more? They broke into the bedroom,
Ulysses with them, the insidious and malignant . . .
O gods, as my plea for vengeance is a just one. Gods!
Retaliate! Strike the Greeks with all due punishment.
But you, what of you? It is time I heard your story:
What turn of events has brought you here alive?
Do you come as a survivor, tempest-tossed,
720   Or at the gods' behest? What destiny hounds you
Down to these sunless, poor abodes, this land
Of troubles?"

Hac vice sermonum roseis Aurora quadrigis
iam medium aetherio cursu traiecerat axem;
et fors omne datum traherent per talia tempus,
sed comes admonuit breviterque adfata Sibylla est:
"nox ruit, Aenea; nos flendo ducimus horas.
540 hic locus est, partis ubi se via findit in ambas:
dextera quae Ditis magni sub moenia tendit,
hac iter Elysium nobis; at laeva malorum
exercet poenas, et ad impia Tartara mittit."
Deiphobus contra: "ne saevi, magna sacerdos;
discedam, explebo numerum reddarque tenebris.
i decus, i, nostrum; melioribus utere fatis."
tantum effatus, et in verbo vestigia torsit.
    Respicit Aeneas subito et sub rupe sinistra
moenia lata videt, triplici circumdata muro,
550 quae rapidus flammis ambit torrentibus amnis,
Tartareus Phlegethon, torquetque sonantia saxa.
porta adversa, ingens, solidoque adamante columnae,

Dawn in her rose-flushed chariot
Had taken her airy drive up half the sky
As they talked together, and in all likelihood
They would have talked on for whatever time
Had been allotted, but that the Sibyl at Aeneas' side
Reproved him in a few brief words. "Night, Aeneas,
Has begun to fall. We are wasting time lamenting.
730   This is the fork of the road, here it divides.
To the right, where it runs beneath the walls
Of mighty Pluto's fortress, that one we take
To Elysium; the one to the left sends evil-doers
To punishment in merciless Tartarus."

                        Deiphobus
Then replied, "Do not, high priestess, be angry.
I will be gone, will take my place with the rest, yield
Once more to the dark. But you, the glory of Troy, go,
Go you to a happier fate."

740   He had said
His say, and as he spoke turned on his heel.

Aeneas suddenly looks back and sees
A broad-based fortress under a cliff to the left,
Set behind three rings of wall, encircled
By a hurtling torrent, a surge and rush of flame,
Rock-rumbling, thunder-flowing Phlegethon, the fiery
Bourne of Tartarus. A gate rears up in front,
Flanked by pillars of solid adamant, so massive

vis ut nulla virum, non ipsi exscindere bello
caelicolae valeant; stat ferrea turris ad auras,
Tisiphoneque sedens, palla succincta cruenta,
vestibulum exsomnis servat noctesque diesque.
hinc exaudiri gemitus, et saeva sonare
verbera, tum stridor ferri tractaeque catenae.
constitit Aeneas strepitumque exterritus hausit.
560 "quae scelerum facies? o virgo, effare: quibusve
urgentur poenis? quis tantus plangor ad auras?"
tum vates sic orsa loqui: "dux inclute Teucrum,
nulli fas casto sceleratum insistere limen;
sed me cum lucis Hecate praefecit Avernis,
ipsa deum poenas docuit perque omnia duxit.
Cnosius haec Rhadamanthus habet durissima regna
castigatque auditque dolos subigitque fateri,
quae quis apud superos, furto laetatus inani,
distulit in seram commissa piacula mortem.
570 continuo sontis ultrix accincta flagello
Tisiphone quatit insultans, torvosque sinistra

No human force, nor even the sky-gods' squadrons

750   Could dislodge them. There too stands an iron tower

And from its top Tisiphone the Fury

Oversees the entrance day and night, unsleeping

And on guard, her bloody dress hitched up.

Sounds of groaning could be heard inside, the savage

Application of the lash, the fling and scringe and drag

Of iron chains. Aeneas stopped short, petrified,

Taking in the turmoil and the shouting,

Then asked the Sibyl: "What wrong-doing

Is being dealt with here? What punishments

760   Afflict the wrong-doers? What is this wailing

High upon the wind?"

                      And the prophetess

Answered him: "Famed chieftain of the Trojans,

Know it is forbidden for the pure in spirit

To set foot on the god-cursed threshold. And yet

When Hecate gave me charge of Avernus' woods

She took me through this whole place and explained

The punishments gods impose. Rhadamanthus

Of Knossos rules here, unforgiving, castigating,

770   Hearing admissions of guilt and exacting

Confession from those self-deceiving souls

Who thought to hide wrongs done in the world above

And left them unatoned for till too late.

Vengeful Tisiphone keeps bearing down, a whiplash

Lapped and lithe in her right hand, in her left

A flail of writhing snakes, scourging the guilty,

intentans anguis vocat agmina saeva sororum.
tum demum horrisono stridentes cardine sacrae
panduntur portae. cernis, custodia qualis
vestibulo sedeat, facies quae limina servet?
quinquaginta atris immanis hiatibus Hydra
saevior intus habet sedem. tum Tartarus ipse
bis patet in praeceps tantum tenditque sub umbras,
quantus ad aetherium caeli suspectus Olympum.
580   hic genus antiquum Terrae, Titania pubes,
fulmine deiecti fundo volvuntur in imo.
hic et Aloidas geminos immania vidi
corpora, qui manibus magnum rescindere caelum
adgressi superisque Iovem detrudere regnis.
vidi et crudelis dantem Salmonea poenas,
dum flammas Iovis et sonitus imitatur Olympi.
quattuor hic invectus equis et lampada quassans
per Graium populos mediaeque per Elidis urbem
ibat ovans, divumque sibi poscebat honorem,
590   demens, qui nimbos et non imitabile fulmen
aere et cornipedum pulsu simularet equorum.

Summoning her ferocious claque of sisters.

Next comes a grinding scrunch and screech

Of hinges as the dread doors open

780 And you see what waits inside, the shape

And threat of the guard who haunts the threshold.

Farther in and more ruthless still, the Hydra lurks,

Monstrous, with her fifty gaping mouth-holes

And black gullets. And beyond, the sheer plunge

Of Tartarus down to the depths, to darkness, a drop

Twice as far beneath the earth as Olympus

Appears to soar above it.

                     In the bottom of the pit,

In the very lowest sump, felled by Jove's thunderbolt,

790 Earth's ancient sons, the Titans, writhe, abased.

Here too I saw the sons of Aloeus, giant twins

Who attempted to grapple with high heaven

And depose the Father of the Skies.

Salmoneus too I saw, paying dear

For having played at being Jupiter, wielding fire

And imitating the thunders of Olympus.

He rode in triumph through the Greek nations

And his own city in Elis, drawn by four horses

And flourishing a torch, assuming to himself

800 The honour due to gods. It was madness:

To think that the batter of bronze and the clatter

Of horses' hoofs could mimic Jupiter's

Absolute thunder and his scowling storms!

But the all-powerful Father—no fake lightning for him

at pater omnipotens densa inter nubila telum
contorsit, non ille faces nec fumea taedis
lumina, praecipitemque immani turbine adegit.
nec non et Tityon, Terrae omniparentis alumnum,
cernere erat, per tota novem cui iugera corpus
porrigitur, rostroque immanis vultur obunco
immortale iecur tondens fecundaque poenis
viscera, rimaturque epulis habitatque sub alto
600   pectore, nec fibris requies datur ulla renatis.
quid memorem Lapithas, Ixiona Pirithoumque et
quo super atra silex iam iam lapsura cadentique
imminet adsimilis? lucent genialibus altis
aurea fulcra toris, epulaeque ante ora paratae
regifico luxu; Furiarum maxima iuxta
accubat et manibus prohibet contingere mensas,
exsurgitque facem attollens atque intonat ore.
        "Hic quibus invisi fratres, dum vita manebat,
pulsatusve parens, et fraus innexa clienti,
610   aut qui divitiis soli incubuere repertis
nec partem posuere suis (quae maxima turba est),

From torches or smoky guttering pine-brands—
Hurled his bright bolt from behind the cloud murk
And blasted Salmoneus headlong down
In an overwhelming whirlwind. There as well
You'd see Tityos, foster-son of Earth,
810   The mother of all. Tityos, his body stretching out
Over nine whole acres while a huge, horrendous
Vulture puddles forever with hooked beak
In his liver and entrails teeming with raw pain.
It burrows deep below the breastbone, feeding
And foraging without respite, for the gnawed-at
Gut and gutstrings keep renewing.

                    And the Lapiths,
Ixion and Parothous, should I mention them?
Eternally menaced by a looming boulder, black
820   And eternally about to fall. Golden headrests
Gleam on their high banquet couches, a sumptuous
Royal feast is spread to tempt them; but nearby
The arch-Fury occupies her place, warding off
Hands that long to reach out to the meal, ever ready
To spring, with her lifted torch and terrifying yells.

"Also incarcerated, those who for a lifetime
Hated a brother, abused a parent, or ruined
The good name of a client; those who gloated
On wealth they'd secretly amassed and hoarded
830   And failed to share with kith and kin (they comprised
The biggest crowd); those killed as adulterers;

quique ob adulterium caesi, quique arma secuti
impia nec veriti dominorum fallere dextras,
inclusi poenam exspectant. ne quaere doceri,
quam poenam, aut quae forma viros fortunave mersit.
saxum ingens volvunt alii, radiisque rotarum
destricti pendent; sedet aeternumque sedebit
infelix Theseus; Phlegyasque miserrimus omnis
admonet et magna testatur voce per umbras:
620   'discite iustitiam moniti et non temnere divos.'
vendidit hic auro patriam dominumque potentem
imposuit; fixit leges pretio atque refixit;
hic thalamum invasit natae vetitosque hymenaeos
ausi omnes immane nefas ausoque potiti.
non mihi si linguae centum sint oraque centum,
ferrea vox, omnis scelerum comprendere formas,
omnia poenarum percurrere nomina possim."

      Haec ubi dicta dedit Phoebi longaeva sacerdos,
"sed iam age, carpe viam et susceptum perfice munus,
630   acceleremus," ait. "Cyclopum educta caminis
moenia conspicio atque adverso fornice portas,
haec ubi nos praecepta iubent deponere dona."

Those who broke oaths of loyalty to masters
In violent rebellions: all were confined there
Awaiting punishment. What that punishment would be,
What fault or fate entailed it, do not seek to know.
Some roll a massive boulder or hang spreadeagled,
Tied to the spokes of wheels. Theseus, unlucky soul,
Sits unmoving and will sit like that forever,
While Phlegyas, most stricken of all, cautions all,
840   A constant proof of what his voice proclaims
Loudly through the darkness: 'Take warning by me;
Learn to do right; learn not to scorn the gods.'
Here too was one who sold his country's freedom,
Leaving her in thrall to a tyrant lord;
Here one who would fix laws for a price and for a price
Unfix them; here another who forced a daughter
In her bed and into an abominable marriage.
All dared to commit great wrong and were fit
For what they dared. If I had a hundred tongues,
850   If I had a hundred mouths and an iron voice,
I could neither spell out the foul catalogue
Of those crimes nor name their punishments."

Here Apollo's venerable priestess paused
Before continuing: "But enough. Be quick. You must
Conclude your undertaking now. We both must hurry.
I see ramparts fashioned in Cyclopic foundries
And gates there in the arch in front of us
Where the powers that be require us to deposit

dixerat, et pariter gressi per opaca viarum
corripiunt spatium medium foribusque propinquant.
occupat Aeneas aditum corpusque recenti
spargit aqua ramumque adverso in limine figit.

His demum exactis, perfecto munere divae,
devenere locos laetos et amoena virecta
Fortunatorum Nemorum sedesque beatas.
640 largior hic campos aether et lumine vestit
purpureo, solemque suum, sua sidera norunt.
pars in gramineis exercent membra palaestris,
contendunt ludo et fulva luctantur harena;
pars pedibus plaudunt choreas et carmina dicunt.
nec non Threicius longa cum veste sacerdos
obloquitur numeris septem discrimina vocum,
iamque fidem digitis, iam pectine pulsat eburno.
hic genus antiquum Teucri, pulcherrima proles,
magnanimi heroes, nati melioribus annis,
650 Ilusque Assaracusque et Troiae Dardanus auctor.
arma procul currusque virum miratur inanis;
stant terra defixae hastae, passimque soluti
per campum pascuntur equi; quae gratia currum
armorumque fuit vivis, quae cura nitentis

Proserpina's gift." That said, they proceed in step

860   Along the dark of pathways, then hurry out

Across the open ground that fronts the doors.

Aeneas takes his stand in the entrance, purifies

His body with fresh water, and there and then

Plants the bough in the threshold.

                                With this ritual

Finally performed and honour done to the goddess,

They came into happy vistas and the green welcome

Of the Groves of the Fortunate Ones who dwell in joy.

Here a more spacious air sheds brightness

870   Over the land; they enjoy their own sun here

And their own stars—some at their exercises

On the grass, some competing in earnest, wrestling

On yellow sand; others are dancing dances

And singing songs, Orpheus among them

In his long musician's robe, keeping time,

Plucking his seven notes from the seven-stringed lyre

Now with his fingers, now with an ivory plectrum.

Here too were members of Teucer's ancient stock,

That noblest of families, magnificent heroes

880   Born in better days—Illus and Assaracus

And Dardanus who founded Troy. Aeneas gazed

In wonder at their armour and the chariots beside them

Standing idle, their spears struck tall in the ground

And their horses loosed out, free to graze the plain

Anywhere they liked. The pride they took when alive

In armour and chariots, the care they gave

pascere equos, eadem sequitur tellure repostos.
conspicit ecce alios dextra laevaque per herbam
vescentis laetumque choro paeana canentis
inter odoratum lauri nemus, unde superne
plurimus Eridani per silvam volvitur amnis.

660   Hic manus ob patriam pugnando vulnera passi,
quique sacerdotes casti, dum vita manebat,
quique pii vates et Phoebo digna locuti,
inventas aut qui vitam excoluere per artes,
quique sui memores aliquos fecere merendo:
omnibus his nivea cinguntur tempora vitta.
quos circumfusos sic est adfata Sibylla,
Musaeum ante omnis; medium nam plurima turba
hunc habet atque umeris exstantem suspicit altis:
"dicite, felices animae, tuque, optime vates,

670   quae regio Anchisen, quis habet locus? illius ergo
venimus et magnos Erebi tranavimus amnis."
atque huic responsum paucis ita reddidit heros:
"nulli certa domus; lucis habitamus opacis
riparumque toros et prata recentia rivis
incolimus. sed vos, si fert ita corde voluntas,
hoc superate iugum, et facili iam tramite sistam."
dixit et ante tulit gressum camposque nitentis
desuper ostentat; dehinc summa cacumina linquunt.

To their glossy well-groomed teams, it is still the same
Now they have gone away under the earth. Others too
He sees on every side, feasting in lush meadows
890   Or singing songs together to Apollo
Deep in a laurel grove, where the Eridanus
Courses through on its way to the earth above.

Here was a band of those who suffered wounds
Fighting for their country; those who lived the pure life
Of the priest; those who were dedicated poets
And made songs fit for Apollo; others still
Whose discoveries improved our arts or ease, and those
Remembered for a life spent serving others—
All of them with headbands white as snow
900   Tied round their brows. These the Sibyl now addressed
As they bustled close around her, Musaeus
In particular, who stood out at the centre of the crowd,
The one looked up to, towering head and shoulders
Over them. "Tell us, happy spirits," she began,
"And you, the best of the poets, tell us
Where does Anchises lodge, in which quarter?
For his sake we have crossed the mighty waterways
To be here." Her question the great hero answered
Briefly: "None of us has one definite home place.
910   We haunt the shadowy woods, bed down on riverbanks,
On meadowland in earshot of running streams.
But you, if your heart is set upon it, climb this ridge
And I'll direct you soon on an easy path." He spoke,
Walked on ahead and showed the fields of light.

　　　　At pater Anchises penitus convalle virenti
680　inclusas animas superumque ad lumen ituras
　　　lustrabat studio recolens, omnemque suorum
　　　forte recensebat numerum carosque nepotes
　　　fataque fortunasque virum moresque manusque.
　　　isque ubi tendentem adversum per gramina vidit
　　　Aenean, alacris palmas utrasque tetendit,
　　　effusaeque genis lacrimae et vox excidit ore:
　　　"venisti tandem, tuaque exspectata parenti
　　　vicit iter durum pietas? datur ora tueri,
　　　nate, tua et notas audire et reddere voces?
690　sic equidem ducebam animo rebarque futurum,
　　　tempora dinumerans, nec me mea cura fefellit.
　　　quas ego te terras et quanta per aequora vectum
　　　accipio! quantis iactatum, nate, periclis!
　　　quam metui, ne quid Libyae tibi regna nocerent!"
　　　ille autem: "tua me, genitor, tua tristis imago
　　　saepius occurrens haec limina tendere adegit;
　　　stant sale Tyrrheno classes. da iungere dextram,

Aeneas and the Sibyl came down the hill.

                            Elsewhere Anchises,

Fatherly and intent, was off in a deep green valley
Surveying and reviewing souls consigned there,
Those due to pass to the light of the upper world.
920   It so happened he was just then taking note
Of his whole posterity, the destinies and doings,
Traits and qualities of descendants dear to him,
But seeing Aeneas come wading through the grass
Towards him, he reached his two hands out
In eager joy, his eyes filled up with tears
And he gave a cry: "At last! Are you here at last?
I always trusted that your sense of right
Would prevail and keep you going to the end.
And am I now allowed to see your face,
930   My son, and hear you talk, and talk to you myself?
This is what I imagined and looked forward to
As I counted the days; and my trust was not misplaced.
To think of the lands and the outlying seas
You have crossed, my son, to receive this welcome.
And after such dangers! I was afraid that Africa
Might be your undoing." But Aeneas replied:
"Often and often, father, you would appear to me,
Your sad shade would appear, and that kept me going
To this end. My ships are anchored in the Tuscan sea.
940   Let me take your hand, my father, O let me, and do not

da, genitor, teque amplexu ne subtrahe nostro."
sic memorans largo fletu simul ora rigabat.
700 ter conatus ibi collo dare bracchia circum,
ter frustra comprensa manus effugit imago,
par levibus ventis volucrique simillima somno.

Interea videt Aeneas in valle reducta
seclusum nemus et virgulta sonantia silvae
Lethaeumque, domos placidas qui praenatat, amnem.
hunc circum innumerae gentes populique volabant;
ac velut in pratis ubi apes aestate serena
floribus insidunt variis et candida circum
lilia funduntur, strepit omnis murmure campus.
710 horrescit visu subito causasque requirit
inscius Aeneas, quae sint ea flumina porro,
quive viri tanto complerint agmine ripas.
tum pater Anchises: "animae, quibus altera fato
corpora debentur, Lethaei ad fluminis undam
securos latices et longa oblivia potant.
has equidem memorare tibi atque ostendere coram,
iampridem hanc prolem cupio enumerare meorum,

Hold back from my embrace." And as he spoke he wept.
Three times he tried to reach arms round that neck.
Three times the form, reached for in vain, escaped
Like a breeze between his hands, a dream on wings.

Meanwhile, at the far end of a valley, Aeneas saw
A remote grove, bushy rustling thickets,
And the river Lethe somnolently flowing,
Lapping those peaceful haunts along its banks.
Here a hovering multitude, innumerable
950　Nations and gathered clans, kept the fields
Humming with life, like bees in meadows
On a clear summer day alighting on pied flowers
And wafting in mazy swarms around white lilies.
Aeneas startled at this unexpected sight
And in his bewilderment asked what was happening,
What was the river drifting past beyond them,
Who were the ones in such a populous throng
Beside it?
　　　　　　"Spirits," Anchises answered,
960　"They are spirits destined to live a second life
In the body; they assemble here to drink
From the brimming Lethe, and its water
Heals their anxieties and obliterates
All trace of memory. For a long time now
I have looked forward to telling you about them,
Letting you see them face to face, but most of all
I wished to call the roll of my descendants, parade

quo magis Italia mecum laetere reperta."

"o pater, anne aliquas ad caelum hinc ire putandum est
720   sublimis animas iterumque ad tarda reverti
corpora? quae lucis miseris tam dira cupido?"
"dicam equidem nec te suspensum, nate, tenebo,"
suscipit Anchises atque ordine singula pandit.

          "Principio caelum ac terras camposque liquentis
lucentemque globum lunae Titaniaque astra
spiritus intus alit, totamque infusa per artus
mens agitat molem et magno se corpore miscet.
inde hominum pecudumque genus vitaeque volantum
et quae marmoreo fert monstra sub aequore pontus.
730   igneus est ollis vigor et caelestis origo
seminibus, quantum non noxia corpora tardant
terrenique hebetant artus moribundaque membra.
hinc metuunt cupiuntque, dolent gaudentque, neque
          auras
dispiciunt clausae tenebris et carcere caeco.
quin et supremo cum lumine vita reliquit,

My children's children, so you could all the more
Share my joy at your landfall in Italia."

970 "Are we to believe then, father, there are souls
Who rise from here to the sky of the upper world
And re-enter the sluggish drag of the body?
What possesses the poor souls? Why this mad desire
To get back to the light?" "To put you out of doubt,"
Anchises answers, "I shall explain it straightaway."
And point by point he then outlines the doctrine.

"To begin at the beginning: a nurturing inner spirit
Works to sustain sky, earth, the fields of ocean,
The moon's bright disc and Titan's star, the sun;
980 And mind, operative in every part, imbues
The massive whole, blending with world's body.
From which are born races of men and beasts,
Creatures that fly, and prodigies ocean breeds
Beneath the molten marble of its surface.
The seeds of life are strong sparks out of fire,
Their origin divine, so to that extent
They are immune to the heavy toll of the body,
Their quickness unaffected by the toil
Of human limbs and the mortal clothing
990 Of the flesh. It is from body
That fear and desire, grief and delight derive,
And in the darkness of its prison house
Those first pure elements are shut off and screened

non tamen omne malum miseris nec funditus omnes
corporeae excedunt pestes, penitusque necesse est
multa diu concreta modis inolescere miris.
ergo exercentur poenis veterumque malorum
740   supplicia expendunt. aliae panduntur inanes
suspensae ad ventos, aliis sub gurgite vasto
infectum eluitur scelus aut exuritur igni,
donec longa dies perfecto temporis orbe
concretam exemit labem, purumque relinquit
aetherium sensum atque aurai simplicis ignem:
quisque suos patimur manis. exinde per amplum
mittimur Elysium et pauci laeta arva tenemus.
has omnis, ubi mille rotam volvere per annos,
Lethaeum ad fluvium deus evocat agmine magno,
750   scilicet immemores supera ut convexa revisant
rursus, et incipiant in corpora velle reverti."

      Dixerat Anchises, natumque unaque Sibyllam
conventus trahit in medios turbamque sonantem,
et tumulum capit unde omnis longo ordine posset

From the light of heaven. Besides which, at the end
When life departs, they remain sadly infested
By every evil and every bodily ill,
For inevitably, in the course of time,
Many flaws mysteriously coalesce, hard set
And deep ingrained. Therefore souls are visited
1000   With due chastisements and affliction, to atone
For past offences. Some are hung racked
And raked by vacuous winds; for others, the stain
Is washed away beneath whirling torrents
Or burnt off in fire. Each of us suffers
The death we're due, then given the freedom
Of broad Elysium—the few, that is, who'll dwell
In those blessèd fields until the end of time
When length of days will remove the deep-dyed taint,
Purify the aethereal sense and that sheer original stuff
1010   Of fire and spirit. The rest, when they have trod
Time's mill for a thousand years, the god commands
Wave upon wave into the Lethe river, so at that stage
Their memory is effaced and they go once more
To dwell beneath sky's dome and start again
To long for the old life of flesh and blood."

Anchises concluded and led his son
Accompanied by the Sibyl into the crowd,
Into the thick and buzzing throb of it,
Then took his stand on a height where he could inspect

adversos legere et venientum discere vultus.

      "Nunc age, Dardaniam prolem quae deinde sequatur
gloria, qui maneant Itala de gente nepotes,
inlustris animas nostrumque in nomen ituras,
expediam dictis, et te tua fata docebo.
760   ille, vides, pura iuvenis qui nititur hasta,
proxima sorte tenet lucis loca, primus ad auras
aetherias Italo commixtus sanguine surget,
Silvius, Albanum nomen, tua postuma proles,
quem tibi longaevo serum Lavinia coniunx
educet silvis regem regumque parentem,
unde genus Longa nostrum dominabitur Alba.
proximus ille Procas, Troianae gloria gentis,
et Capys et Numitor et qui te nomine reddet
Silvius Aeneas, pariter pietate vel armis
770   egregius, si umquam regnandam acceperit Albam.
qui iuvenes! quantas ostentant, aspice, vires
atque umbrata gerunt civili tempora quercu!
hi tibi Nomentum et Gabios urbemque Fidenam,
hi Collatinas imponent montibus arces,
Pometios Castrumque Inui Bolamque Coramque;

1020　The long, drawn-out procession and take note
　　　　Of every face as it approached and passed.

　　　　"So now I will instruct you in what is to be,
　　　　The future glory of the Trojan race,
　　　　Descendants due to be born in Italia,
　　　　Souls who in time will make our name illustrious—
　　　　I speak of them to reveal your destiny to you.
　　　　The lad you see there, who leans on his untipped spear,
　　　　Placed next and nearest to the light, he will be
　　　　The first to ascend to upper air, the first
1030　Of our people with mixed Italian blood.
　　　　He'll be known as Silvius, an Alban name,
　　　　And be the last of your children; when you are old
　　　　Your wife Lavinia will rear him in the woods
　　　　To be a king and to father kings our stock
　　　　Will issue from and rule in Alba Longa.
　　　　Next to him stands Procas, pride and joy
　　　　Of the Trojan nation, then Capys and Numitor
　　　　And the one in whose name you will survive, Silvius
　　　　Aeneas, no less distinguished as a warrior than you
1040　And no less devoted, though he'll be waiting long
　　　　To rule in Alba. Look at them! Marvellous, strong
　　　　Young men, wearing their civic honours, oak wreaths
　　　　Like shadowy crowns. These, when you are gone,
　　　　Will build Nomentum and Gabii and the city of Fidena,
　　　　Fortify hill towns, wall the citadels
　　　　Of Collatia, found Pometii, Bola and Cora

haec tum nomina erunt, nunc sunt sine nomine terrae.

quin et avo comitem sese Mavortius addet

Romulus, Assaraci quem sanguinis Ilia mater

educet. viden, ut geminae stant vertice cristae

780   et pater ipse suo superum iam signat honore?

en huius, nate, auspiciis illa incluta Roma

imperium terris, animos aequabit Olympo,

septemque una sibi muro circumdabit arces,

felix prole virum: qualis Berecyntia mater

invehitur curru Phrygias turrita per urbes

laeta deum partu, centum complexa nepotes,

omnis caelicolas, omnis supera alta tenentis.

    "Huc geminas nunc flecte acies, hanc aspice gentem

Romanosque tuos. hic Caesar et omnis Iuli

790   progenies magnum caeli ventura sub axem.

hic vir, hic est, tibi quem promitti saepius audis,

Augustus Caesar, divi genus, aurea condet

saecula qui rursus Latio regnata per arva

Saturno quondam, super et Garamantas et Indos

And Camp Inuus: unheard-of today, unsignified,
Their name and fame will come. And Romulus, yes,
Son of Mars, grandson of Numitor, whom Illia
1050   Is to bear, Romulus will stand firm by his grandfather.
Do you see how the twin plumes wave above his head,
How the Father of the gods has marked him out
With his own insignia for singular majesty?
Once he inaugurates the power of Rome,
She in her glory will push an empire's bounds
To the ends of earth and harbour aspirations
High as heaven; seven hills she will girdle with a wall
Into a single city and be blessed with heroic sons.
She will be like Cybele with her crown of towers,
1060   The Great Mother borne in her chariot
Through the cities of Phrygia, happy and fulfilled
To have given birth to gods, grandchildren
By the score in her generous arms,
All of them sky-dwellers, tenants of the heights.

"Now look this way, take good note of this clan,
Your own bloodline in Rome: there is Caesar
And the whole offspring of Iulus, destined one day
To issue forth beneath the dome of heaven.
This is he whose coming you've heard foretold
1070   So often: Augustus Caesar, child of the divine one,
Who will establish in Latium, in Saturn's old domain,
A second golden age. He will advance his empire
Beyond the Garamants and the Indians

proferet imperium; iacet extra sidera tellus,
extra anni solisque vias, ubi caelifer Atlas
axem umero torquet stellis ardentibus aptum.
huius in adventum iam nunc et Caspia regna
responsis horrent divum et Maeotia tellus,
800 et septemgemini turbant trepida ostia Nili.
nec vero Alcides tantum telluris obivit,
fixerit aeripedem cervam licet, aut Erymanthi
pacarit nemora et Lernam tremefecerit arcu;
nec qui pampineis victor iuga flectit habenis
Liber, agens celso Nysae de vertice tigris.
et dubitamus adhuc virtutem extendere factis,
aut metus Ausonia prohibet consistere terra?
        "Quis procul ille autem ramis insignis olivae
sacra ferens? nosco crinis incanaque menta
810 regis Romani primam qui legibus urbem
fundabit, Curibus parvis et paupere terra
missus in imperium magnum. cui deinde subibit
otia qui rumpet patriae residesque movebit
Tullus in arma viros et iam desueta triumphis

To lands unseen beneath our constellations
Beyond the sun's path through the zodiac,
Away where sky-braced Atlas pivots on his shoulder
The firmament, inlaid with glittering stars.
Already the Caspian kingdoms and Maeotia
Know of his coming and begin to tremble
1080   At the oracles of their gods; the waters of the Nile
Quail in alarm and roil through their seven mouths.
Not even Hercules pursued his labours over
So much of earth's surface, not when he stalked
And shot the bronze-toed deer, silenced the boar
In the woods of Erymanthus and left the air of Lerna
Vibrating to his bowstring; not Bacchus either
Careering in triumph, the vine-reins in his grip,
Driving his tiger team down the heights of Nysa.
So why should we then hesitate to test
1090   And prove our worth in action or be afraid
To stake and stand our ground in Italia?

"But that one in the crown of olive sprays,
Offering sacrifice—that grey head
And grizzled beard I recognise as Numa's,
King of Rome, sprung from the humble town
Of Cures, called from its poor land to wield high power
And frame the city's first system of laws.
To be succeeded next by Tullus, who will wreck
His country's peace, turn an easygoing people
1100   Militant and drill an army long out of the field

agmina. quem iuxta sequitur iactantior Ancus
nunc quoque iam nimium gaudens popularibus auris.
vis et Tarquinios reges animamque superbam
ultoris Bruti, fascesque videre receptos?
consulis imperium hic primus saevasque secures
820 accipiet, natosque pater nova bella moventis
ad poenam pulchra pro libertate vocabit,
infelix, utcumque ferent ea facta minores:
vincet amor patriae laudumque immensa cupido.

   "Quin Decios Drusosque procul saevumque securi
aspice Torquatum et referentem signa Camillum.
illae autem, paribus quas fulgere cernis in armis,
concordes animae nunc et dum nocte prementur,
heu quantum inter se bellum, si lumina vitae
attigerint, quantas acies stragemque ciebunt,
830 aggeribus socer Alpinis atque arce Monoeci
descendens, gener adversis instructus Eois!

For victory. After him, that's Ancus, swaggering,
Too full of himself already, overly susceptible
To the wind of popularity in his sails.
And there, if you care to look, are the regal Tarquins
And haughty Brutus, called Avenger, who'll arrange
The handover of the fasces—first consul
To be installed and given authority
As custodian of the pitiless axes.
Then as a father, when his sons foment their plot,
1110 He will decree their summary execution
In the fair name of liberty—stricken in this
No matter how future generations may comprehend it:
Love of country will prevail and the overwhelming
Desire for fame.

            "Now over there you see
The Decii and the Drusi, Torquatus who will behead
His son, and Camillus who'll recapture the standards.
But alas for that pair in their burnished armour,
Well-matched champions, twin souls in accord
1120 As long as they stay pent in this shadowland,
But once promoted to the light above
What mutual destruction they will wreak,
The internecine savagery and slaughter
Of a civil war: Caesar, the bride's father,
Bearing down from the northern Alps,
Pompey, the husband, with his legions in formation
Advancing from the east. Do not, O my sons,

ne, pueri, ne tanta animis adsuescite bella
neu patriae validas in viscera vertite vires;
tuque prior, tu parce, genus qui ducis Olympo,
proice tela manu, sanguis meus! . . .
     "Ille triumphata Capitolia ad alta Corintho
victor aget currum caesis insignis Achivis.
eruet ille Argos Agamemnoniasque Mycenas
ipsumque Aeaciden, genus armipotentis Achilli,
840 ultus avos Troiae templa et temerata Minervae.
quis te, magne Cato, tacitum aut te, Cosse, relinquat?
quis Gracchi genus aut geminos, duo fulmina belli,
Scipiadas, cladem Libyae, parvoque potentem
Fabricium vel te sulco, Serrane, serentem?
quo fessum rapitis, Fabii? tu Maximus ille es,
unus qui nobis cunctando restituis rem.
excudent alii spirantia mollius aera
(credo equidem), vivos ducent de marmore vultus,
orabunt causas melius, caelique meatus

Inure yourselves to such dreadful consequence, do not

Bloody the bosom of your country with vicious,

1130   Valiant battle. And you, child of my blood,

Of the gods on high Olympus, be you the first

In clemency: rid your hands of those weapons.

"Yonder too is Mummius, conqueror

Of Corinth, who will ride his victor's chariot

Up to the Capitol, a hero for having brought

Ruination on the Greeks. That other at his side

Will destroy Argos and Agamemnon's Mycenae,

Defeat descendants of arch-warrior Achilles,

Avenge his Trojan forebears and the rape

1140   Of Cassandra in Minerva's temple.

Next, great Cato, you, who could not sing your praise

Or, Cossus, yours? Or the family of the Gracchi;

Or those two Scipios, two warrior thunderbolts

Who will strike down bellicose Carthage; or Fabricius,

The indomitable and frugal; or you, Serranus,

Sowing your furrowed fields? Nor is there a quick

Or easy way to scan the long line of the Fabii,

Down to the greatest, Fabius Maximus,

He who'll contrive to stall and thereby save our state.

1150   Others, I have no doubt, with a more delicate touch

Will beat bronze into breathing likenesses,

Conjure living features out of marble,

Argue cases more effectively, and with their compass

Plot the heavens' orbit and predict

850   describent radio et surgentia sidera dicent:

tu regere imperio populos, Romane, memento

(hae tibi erunt artes), pacique imponere morem,

parcere subiectis et debellare superbos."

    Sic pater Anchises, atque haec mirantibus addit:

"aspice, ut insignis spoliis Marcellus opimis

ingreditur victorque viros supereminet omnis.

hic rem Romanam magno turbante tumultu

sistet, eques sternet Poenos Gallumque rebellem,

tertiaque arma patri suspendet capta Quirino."

860   Atque hic Aeneas (una namque ire videbat

egregium forma iuvenem et fulgentibus armis,

sed frons laeta parum et deiecto lumina vultu)

"quis, pater, ille, virum qui sic comitatur euntem?

filius, anne aliquis magna de stirpe nepotum?

qui strepitus circa comitum! quantum instar in ipso!

sed nox atra caput tristi circumvolat umbra."

    Tum pater Anchises lacrimis ingressus obortis:

"o gnate, ingentem luctum ne quaere tuorum;

ostendent terris hunc tantum fata nec ultra

The rising of the constellations. But you, Roman,
Remember: to you will fall the exercise of power
Over the nations, and these will be your gifts—
To impose peace and justify your sway,
Spare those you conquer, crush those who overbear."

1160   Here Anchises paused; then, while they wondered
At his words, continued: "Look now, there goes
Marcellus, head and shoulders above all the rest,
Victorious in armour of the general he killed.
He will help Rome to stand firm while it bears the brunt
Of fierce invasion, he will ride high over
Carthaginians and insurgent Gauls, then dedicate
Those rich, rare spoils won only twice before
To Father Quirinus."
                              At which point Aeneas saw
1170   A young man in step with Marcellus, arrayed
In glittering arms, exceedingly handsome
But with lowered eyes, unhappy looking, so he asked,
"Who, father, is that companion at his side?
A son, or another of his great descendants?
What crowds and clamour follow him! What presence
He has! But black night wreathes his brow
With dolorous shadow."
                              Choking back his tears,
Anchises answered, "Do not, O my son,
1180   Seek foreknowledge of the heavy sorrow
Your people will endure. Fate will allow the world

870   esse sinent. nimium vobis Romana propago
      visa potens, superi, propria haec si dona fuissent.
      quantos ille virum magnam Mavortis ad urbem
      campus aget gemitus! vel quae, Tiberine, videbis
      funera, cum tumulum praeterlabere recentem!
      nec puer Iliaca quisquam de gente Latinos
      in tantum spe tollet avos, nec Romula quondam
      ullo se tantum tellus iactabit alumno.
      heu pietas, heu prisca fides invictaque bello
      dextera! non illi se quisquam impune tulisset
880   obvius armato, seu cum pedes iret in hostem
      seu spumantis equi foderet calcaribus armos.
      heu, miserande puer, si qua fata aspera rumpas!
      tu Marcellus eris. manibus date lilia plenis
      purpureos spargam flores animamque nepotis
      his saltem accumulem donis, et fungar inani
      munere." sic tota passim regione vagantur
      aëris in campis latis atque omnia lustrant.
      quae postquam Anchises natum per singula duxit
      incenditque animum famae venientis amore,
890   exim bella viro memorat quae deinde gerenda,

Only to glimpse him, then rob it of him quickly.
It's as if the gods decided the Roman people
Would be manifestly too powerful, were the gift
Of his life to last. How the city will re-echo
Massed laments from the brave on the Field of Mars!
What a funeral procession, Tiber, you will witness
As you go flowing past the new built tomb!
No boy born from our Trojan stock will ever raise
1190   The hopes of his Latin ancestors so high
Nor the land of Romulus take such pride in a son.
Alas for his goodness! His antique loyalties!
His strong right arm unbeaten in the battle!
No foe would have faced and fought him and survived,
Whether he marched on foot or sank his spurs
In the flanks of some foaming, lathering warhorse.
O son of pity! Alas that you cannot strike
Fate's cruel fetters off! For you are to be Marcellus . . .
Load my arms with lilies, let me scatter
1200   Purple flowers, let me lavish these gifts at least
On the soul of my inheritor and perform
My unavailing duty."
                And so
Far and wide in those fields, through regions of air,
They go wandering at will, surveying all.
Then after Anchises has conducted Aeneas
Across the whole expanse, scene after scene,
And fired his mind with promise of future glory,
He tells of wars that will first have to be waged,

Laurentisque docet populos urbemque Latini,
et quo quemque modo fugiatque feratque laborem.

  Sunt geminae Somni portae, quarum altera fertur
cornea, qua veris facilis datur exitus umbris,
altera candenti perfecta nitens elephanto,
sed falsa ad caelum mittunt insomnia Manes.
his ibi tum natum Anchises unaque Sibyllam
prosequitur dictis portaque emittit eburna:
ille viam secat ad navis sociosque revisit;
900 tum se ad Caietae recto fert litore portum.
ancora de prora iacitur; stant litore puppes.

1210   Of the Laurentines and the town of King Latinus,
        How he should face or flee each undertaking.

        There are two gates of Sleep, one of which, they say,
        Is made of horn and offers easy passage
        To true visions; the other has a luminous, dense
        Ivory sheen, but through it, to the sky above,
        The spirits of the dead send up false dreams.
        Anchises, still guiding and discoursing,
        Escorts his son and the Sibyl on their way
        And lets them both out by the ivory gate.
1220   Aeneas hurries to the ships and rejoins his comrades,
        Then sails, hugging the shore, to the port of Caietae.
        Anchors are cast from the prow; sterns cushion on sand.

A NOTE ON THE TEXT

For the contemporary reader, it is the best of books and
the worst of books. Best because of its mythopoeic visions,
the twilit fetch of its language, the pathos of the many
encounters it allows the living Aeneas with his familiar
dead. Worst because of its imperial certitude, its celebra-
tion of Rome's manifest destiny and the catalogue of
Roman heroes . . .

With these words Seamus Heaney began what he may have
intended to serve as an afterword to *Aeneid* Book VI. Marked
"Katabasis, Eschatological" (the terms describe the final journey
of the spirit into the underworld), it was the last element that
he introduced to the text. He did not complete it and it re-
mains a tantalising fragment; but he had, by then, completed
a translation of Book VI in its entirety that, in July 2013, he
marked "final" in preparation for showing to his publisher. That
typescript was still in his keeping on his death one month later.

It contained two full-length drafts, as well as pages of rough working; and although one draft was clearly more advanced than the other, the presence of a second version made necessary the task of confirming that the work was indeed "final" as Seamus intended. That search involved comparing a number of annotated and undated typescripts, as well as preliminary proofs for a limited, letterpress edition that he had been exploring with the Bonnefant Press in the Netherlands, in collaboration with the artist Jan Hendrix. From these documents and the accompanying correspondence, it has been possible to arrive at the text for this edition.

Seamus had largely settled the first 1064 lines of his translation by the time he saw a full-length letterpress proof from Bonnefant in 2011; that proof forms the basis of the text here, augmented by a small number of author amendments where they appeared as definitive instructions. The concluding sections of the poem, however—beyond line 1065—continued to be reworked in typescript after that proof had been corrected, and it is for this reason that the last typescript becomes the preferred text from this point onward. The Translator's Note was prepared in two drafts of 2010.

This translation of 1222 lines is Seamus's complete rendering of Book VI, which has 901 lines in the original Latin: it follows the author's latest instructions, and contains no editorial interventions beyond the correction of literals. It seems likely that both poem and note would have received further revision had Seamus seen production through to completion, and in that respect, the author's use of the word "final" may be considered a more precise description of the text than "finished," as well as one in keeping with the *Aeneid*'s own halted composition.

On behalf of the family and the publisher, our heartfelt gratitude extends to those trusted readers who advised Seamus on his translation, and to those who helped to assure us of the virtue of posthumous publication. Our thanks go also to the Bonnefant Press: to Jan Hendrix and publisher Hans van Eijk, for what Seamus described as "an old friendship of artist, printer and poet."

Catherine Heaney
Matthew Hollis